BRAIN STORM

Living with an Acoustic Neuroma Brain Tumor

LISA PORISCH

BRAIN STORM

Living with an Acoustic Neuroma Brain Tumor

Lisa Porisch

LP-Publishing.com

Copyright 2023 Lisa Porisch

ISBN: 979-8-9891072-0-9

Lisa Porisch

3421 W Main Street

Rapid City, SD 57702

(605) 468 1865

lisaporisch@gmail.com

www.LP-Publishing.com

Lisa Porisch is a licensed professional mental health counselor and registered play therapist supervisor with over twenty years of experience working with individuals and families. She was diagnosed with an acoustic neuroma in March 2022, and she underwent brain surgery to have the tumor removed in August 2022.

This book helps define aspects of acoustic neuroma, treatment options, and her journey on the winding path of trying to find balance again after brain surgery.

In 2022, after Lisa was diagnosed with Covid, she was diagnosed with a brain tumor. This captivating story begins with ringing of the inner ear that did not stop after Covid. Lisa went on to learn that she had a rare brain tumor called an acoustic neuroma. What started as an exceedingly difficult journey brought out the best in friends, family, acquaintances, and an entire community. This major life event helps highlight the good in the world and human connection.

Preface

I was diagnosed with a rare brain tumor called an acoustic neuroma (AN) in 2022. I searched for a memoir written by another acoustic neuroma warrior to help me navigate through the decisions and treatment of this tumor. However, I had difficulty finding a memoir that focused mainly on finding balance again after an acoustic neuroma. I wrote this book in late 2023 to help others journey the path after discovering an acoustic neuroma.

My book highlights finding a different path when old patterns prove to be unhelpful. This book will help you learn how to focus on your strengths to create a successful future, no matter what obstacle or hardship has been set in your way.

Timeline of Events

Nov 2021
- Ringing in ears began

Jan 20 2022
- COVID 19+

Mar 14 2022
- Acoustic neuroma diagnosis

Aug 16 2022
- Brain surgery

Aug 18 2022
- Released from hospital to campus housing

Aug 25 2022
- Flew back home

Aug 16 2023
- One year out from surgery

Aug 16 2024
- Two years out from surgery (recovery period basically complete)

Contents

Introduction

I t was a difficult chapter in my life.

I was in the room alone, waiting to be wheeled into the operating room at the University of California in San Diego, a large university-based hospital. The nurse who entered the room was trying to make a personal connection with me by explaining that she was also from the Midwest. She told me not to put my belongings except in the bag provided due to germs. My anxiety was starting to increase very quickly, and I had to practice deep breathing and work on identifying and changing my anxious thoughts. I felt like I was on a roller-coaster ride with the cars carrying frightened, eager, sad, hopeful, and numb along for the ride. I was trying not to go off the track. It was the day and moment I had been waiting for and dreading since the brain tumor diagnosis five months ago.

I knew my husband was waiting in the large waiting room of the hospital for skull-based surgeries. My children were with my parents across the bridge at the college-hospital campus apartments. Everyone was waiting for the brain surgery to be complete. I held in my mind that hundreds of friends, relatives, and acquaintances were praying for me and sending positive thoughts through the miles for a successful removal of the tumor.

The hospital had bright lights and an array of sounds of beds being wheeled, doctors and nurses talking to one another, and machines beeping. I was given an electrocardiogram (EKG) in the pre-operation room to make sure my heart was strong enough to undergo this type of surgery. The young anesthesiologist was stunning with her long braids and beautiful face as she described the next steps in preparing me for the craniotomy. I had a tough time believing she was old enough to be an anesthesiologist, but I was now forty-six, and there were many professionals much younger than I was. There was something very calming about her presence. I felt like I was in a daze. As I was wheeled down to the operating room in a bed covered with white sheets and blankets, I remember them asking me if I would like a warm blanket, and I willingly took this item of comfort since my body was feeling cold in the hospital gown and the air conditioning. I started feeling a sense of warmth and security. I was sinking into my cocoon, and the thought entered my mind that *I would be fine.* I put on the non-slip hospital socks provided, taking off the soft socks my friend Nicci gave me before leaving my hometown to head to California. It was time for *out with the old and in with the new.* However, I had been warned that it would be a long road to improvement. I had many surgeries in the past, but this would be the most difficult recovery. I would wake up in a worse state than when I went under anesthesia. I had to keep my eye on the prize. A year down the road, I would hopefully be feeling better, and the tumor would be a thing of the past.

I felt like I was now part of the hospital microcosm and had officially crossed the bridge into the unknown. The bridge ushered me into this new world. Would I still have my smile when I awoke? Would I relearn to walk and balance this outer shell I have inhabited for forty-some years? Would I adjust to the sensory and balance issues I had been educated about? Would socializing in crowded places be tolerable again at some point? Would I be constantly nauseous and disabled? It was a gamble I had decided to take to rid myself of this brain tumor. There were no guarantees, but I had faith that I would come out alive and kicking on the other side.

I was wheeled down the long hallways and pushed through the double doors to the operating room. I had spent months planning to have this acoustic neuroma that was on my eighth cranial nerve removed. The operation would be on the eighth cranial nerve that connects the ear to the brain. There would also be a piece of flesh surgically removed from my waist and then used to repair and fill the access hole in my skull. They call this a "fat plug" (abdominal fat harvest), which made me chuckle. Into the area of my brain, they would take flesh from my waist to help fill the hole and incision in my skull. This is a bit humorous. I had always wanted less fat on my waist.

There would also be titanium mesh inserted where the tumor would be removed. This created more support and structure for such a delicate and intricately woven organ in the body. I imagined that the titanium mesh would help hold everything back together like a net. There was no turning back now.

I was transferred up onto the operating table on the count of three, with many doctors and assistants working together to lift me in unison. I was fastened down with many contraptions, the room turned fuzzy, and I felt warm all over. I was no longer able to think or feel anything. This was now completely in the hands of skilled surgeons and a higher power. I had to completely let go of all control.

I would wake up several hours later with the brain tumor (acoustic neuroma) removed and gauze wrapped around my skull. I saw my loved ones standing around my hospital bed. I was in a different room and had no recollection of being transported there. It felt like a time machine, where I had lost a number of hours in my life and crossed the threshold. My thoughts were still very fuzzy, but I was ecstatic to see my loved ones beside me, knowing they would do everything in their power to help me along the way. I was alive! I could see the room around me with my eyes and speak with my mouth.

The surgical team had safely brought me to the other side of brain surgery! I may not have felt strong that morning in the hospital, but the surgical team and my family were a pillar of strength guiding me through this journey. I borrowed their strength until I could find mine again.

Making it through brain surgery would always be a part of me and my new story. If I could make it through this predicament, I felt pretty confident I could navigate through most future obstacles.

PART ONE

CHAPTER 1

The Discovery

The Covid pandemic of 2020 had been a stressful time. I had just bought a new building for my counseling practice and was leaving a group I had been a part of for many years and going out on my own. My father had started a group practice that I had left. He had retired a few years prior, and I was looking for a change of pace with my own business.

Regarding family and parenting, my husband and I had numerous emotional conversations about what each of us considered safe activities when discussing pandemic safety for our kids. It started to sound like a broken record, with each of us stating our views. My husband and I were both on board that masks were good, but my husband wanted our youngest son to be in wrestling that year. Our youngest was a good wrestler, and we had never worried too much about health until the airborne virus Covid came into our world. We had differing views and quite a few arguments regarding what would be best for our kids to keep them and the rest of the family safe. My husband stated that he thought everyone in our immediate family would be fine and recuperate if they got Covid. I was more conservative in my views. I had been through a number of odd medical issues in my life and knew how these made life more difficult.

Adding to this, I worked with children every day in my counseling and play therapy practice who have had hard things happen at an early age. I was quite protective of my children. I certainly had seen my fair share of times when things did not turn out well, but I also knew that you can be overprotective as a parent, which is not helpful either. People need to live their lives. Finding the balance was difficult. This was probably a common argument in most households during the height of the pandemic. We also wanted to keep my elderly parents healthy since we saw them often, and children could not be vaccinated at that point when we were discussing pandemic safety for our family. We focused on keeping the younger and older generations safe during this strange time in our world's history. My parents loved seeing my sons and vice versa, but we kept our distance during the pandemic to be mindful of health for all, young and old.

In January 2022, I contracted Covid. Ringing in my left inner ear began with the Covid diagnosis and did not stop. Even after I tested negative for Covid, the ringing continued. I was confused by this and asked other people if they had heard of others having similar symptoms after having Covid. My doctor sent me to an ear, nose, and throat (ENT) clinic.

Initially, the audiologist assessed my hearing in both ears by administering a hearing test. I then met with the physician's assistant at the ENT clinic because she could get me in sooner for an appointment with her than to see one of the doctors. She seemed truly knowledgeable, considering all my symptoms, explaining that I may want to get a magnetic resonance imaging (MRI) scan of my head to rule out a rare type of brain tumor. She stated that it was unlikely because these tumors only occur in about one in 100,000 people. I had been treated for presumed repeated ear infections in my left ear leading up to January. The hearing test that day revealed less sensitivity in my left ear. We decided that it would make sense to get the MRI and rule out this rare brain tumor, and then we would decide where to go from there.

I had never experienced an MRI, at least that I could remember. I was in a car accident when I was only four months old and broke both of my legs. The medical team thought I had "water on the brain," but the MRI had barely been invented at that time. This was the 1970s before car seats were widely used, and a car ran a flashing red light and T-boned our family car. The story I heard was that I hit the windshield, and I was lucky to be alive. I have a photo of me with my legs pointing up toward the ceiling in casts from my hospitalization.

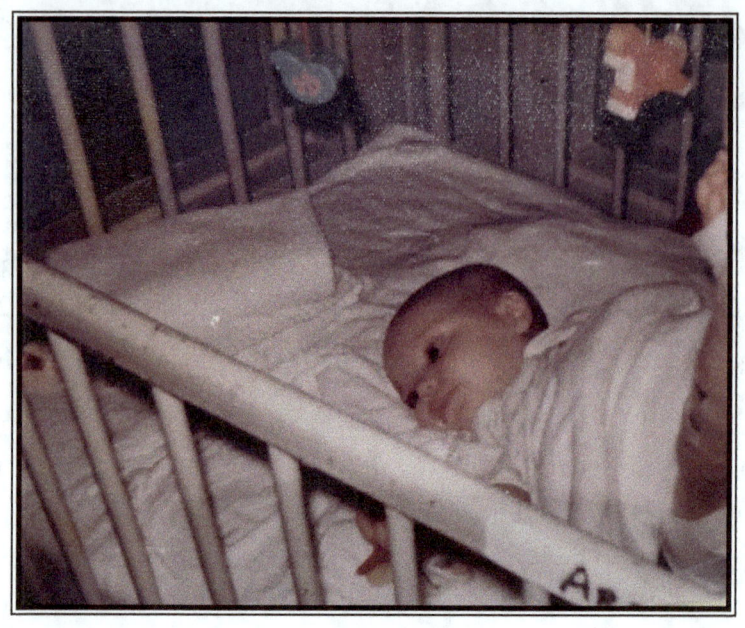

The year was 1976. I was in the hospital for about three weeks. My mother had to abruptly stop breastfeeding due to her injuries and my hospitalization. She has permanent scars on her forehead from the glass of the windshield. My father had a concussion and was hospitalized at a neighboring hospital. What an event to have happened to a four-month-old baby and her family. My mom felt horrible about this and always suggested we help buy car seats for any friends who have been expecting a baby throughout my lifetime. I include this because a genetic abnormality can cause acoustic neuromas, but also from radiation exposure, which may have occurred due to this head trauma with this hospitalization as a baby. Most of the time, though, acoustic neuroma originates from over-activity in the production of Schwann cells on the myelin sheath surrounding the vestibulocochlear nerve.

As an adult, I found the MRI idea frightening, and when they offered anxiety medication, I agreed since I have felt claustrophobic at times. My mother accompanied me to the appointment since I had taken the anxiety medication and they recommended that I did not drive. My mother was very supportive, and we both agreed that it made sense to rule out this rare brain tumor to move forward—a formality. The staff at the imaging center was so kind and considerate. People gave me kind looks that said, "Oh no," since I needed an MRI of my head and brain. The nurse inserted an intravenous (IV) needle into my arm for contrast dye. I was told to lie on a flat white surface of the MRI machine. The plank electronically slid into the machine like a conveyor belt. I was offered headphones and a choice of music to listen to during the MRI. A large contraption was put on my head to keep it in place for imaging, and I was told there would be very loud noises and lights, and I would need to lie as still as possible. They would stop in the middle of the procedure and tell me when they would inject dye into my veins to see the structures more clearly in my brain. I was happy that I could complete this test without panicking. I can sometimes be anxious in enclosed spaces. I kept telling myself that I would be okay and to focus on my slow, controlled breathing to stay calm in this enclosed space. The loud noises sounded like large dumpsters crashing together repeatedly. I was proud that I had made it through this procedure. I thought it would be a one-time experience, but it turned out to be the first of many. Getting MRIs of my head would become a routine experience. I would learn to tolerate many medical procedures as I did this first MRI.

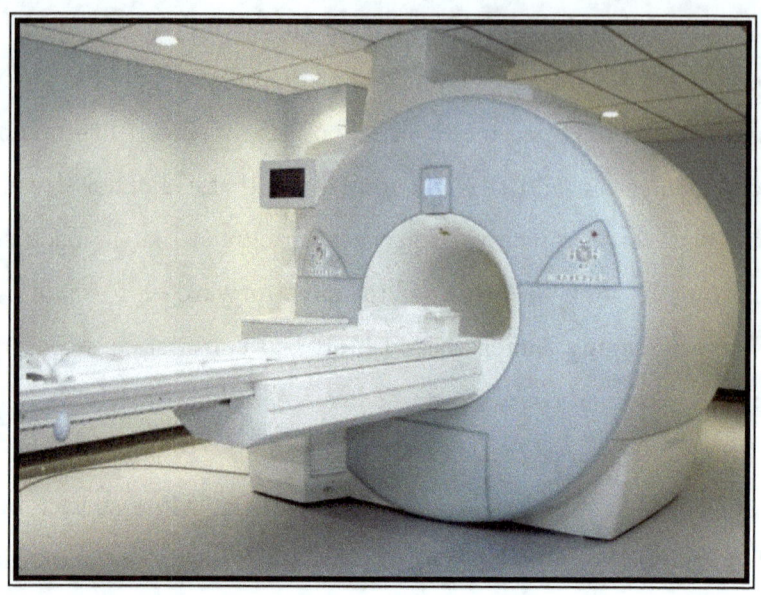

MRI Machine

After more appointments, I received a telephone call from the physician's assistant from the ENT clinic stating that I *did indeed* have a rare brain tumor called an acoustic neuroma or, more specifically, a vestibular schwannoma. It was on my right side, not my symptomatic left side. The tumor was not cancerous, but due to its inconvenient location, it caused hearing loss, balance issues, ringing in the ears (tinnitus), fullness in the ear that feels like an ear infection, and if it grew large, it could be life-threatening. This did not seem real to me. I thought it was some mistake. The phone call ended and I sat there feeling numb. I was unsure what to do, so I continued my normal work day. It was actually a relief to focus the rest of the day on what my clients were experiencing instead of thinking about my situation.

At church that Wednesday evening, I told one of my friends at dinner that I had a brain tumor. She is a school counselor and looked at me like she was shocked. I was laughing as I told her (in disbelief) while tears slid down my face. What a mess of intense emotions I was dealing with. It took quite a bit of time to accept that this was my new reality. I kept repeating to myself, *I have a brain tumor.* This did not seem like it could actually be true, but it was the new reality.

Around the same time I was diagnosed with the tumor, I also started having skin lesions on my torso and armpits. These skin lesions started out red and turned deep brown like leopard spots. It was like nothing I had ever seen before. I was seeing a dermatologist for this, but I put it on the back burner until the brain surgery was over. Around this same time, I also went to the emergency room (ER) because of bleeding from my colon. I woke up in the middle of the night and was vomiting and had massive amounts of blood and chunks of skin in the toilet bowl. It was very alarming. The ER team did not figure out what this was but referred me to a gastrointestinal doctor. After seeing the gastrointestinal doctor, I was told I could immediately get in with him as an established patient if I had another episode. At this point, I wondered what was happening to my brain and body and why. I wanted to say politely, "I will just take the brain tumor. That will be enough for me, thank you." It felt like my body was deteriorating.

When I was diagnosed with the brain tumor, my perspective of the world changed overnight. I felt like I was in the middle of achieving my professional goals and raising my children. There was constantly something that needed to be done and checked off my always-increasing daily list. After learning of the tumor and wondering about the future, I started focusing more on what I wanted to experience and the parts of life that felt most meaningful. If I had a brain tumor, I wanted to go do and see things, travel, and spend time with people that were important to me. No more putting off the good stuff for when I was older, more financially secure, or retired. I wanted to experience more of the meaningful moments in life and less of the busy work. I was not sure about my future and how this would all end. Have you ever faced a sudden life-altering event? How did you learn to accept the news, and how did it change your perspective?

I will share how shifting your perspective can turn adversity into an opportunity for self-actualization, the realization or fulfillment of one's talents. This is considered a need or drive present in everyone. When a hardship occurs, one may change patterns and look to discover the true meaning of life. You may look at your life differently and dig deeper for new experiences, the true meaning of life, change, and connection. It was hard to believe that I really had this brain tumor, but accepting this fact became a catalyst for transformation. I had a lot of life left to live fully. I had been in the preparation phase for many years to create a fulfilling career and a family. It was now time to live this life because my life could be shortened dramatically. Even if I made it through surgery fine, my quality of life could be greatly compromised after surgery.

We have two lives, and the second begins when we realize we only have one.

-Confucius

How do I want to spend my time and energy? There is only a certain amount of time. There are many things I spend time on during the day that I do not find fulfilling. I do these tasks because they are responsibilities or simply must be done. I will continue having responsibilities, but I began spending more time thinking about what I wanted to add to my life and what was most meaningful. So, my new outlook on life began. How would I want to spend my time if I only had months or a few years to be here on earth or fully functioning?

- I planned a trip with my old college friend, whom I do not get to see very often.

- I read many books since I thoroughly enjoy reading and taking myself to other places through books.

- I took training in transcendental meditation to help reduce my anxiety, improve my sleep, and reduce the ringing in my ear.

- I planned a vacation because my children are growing up quickly, and some of our best memories are from family vacations.

- I started to notice more of the positives in my life instead of what needed to be fixed.

- I dove into the moment, learning to thoroughly enjoy the little things, such as a hug from my child or a walk with my dog.

- I spent more time driving around in my convertible, noticing the canyons, streams, and sunshine.

- I focused on making some relationships in my life more positive and noticing the positive in others.

- I tried to let go of what I could not control.

"You know all those things you always wanted to do?"

"You should go and do them."

-E. J. Lamprey

Have you ever turned adversity into moments of personal growth?

How did you go about this transformation?

What did you learn from your adversity improved your life?

CHAPTER 2

Adapting to Life's Unforeseen Turns

The most immediate obstacle I was facing with my acoustic neuroma was the worsening of my quality of life. I had been getting dizzy, sleeping an hour or two in the middle of the day or after work when the ringing became too loud to tolerate. The ringing would be quieter in the morning, and the volume would increase as the day progressed. If I was doing something quiet and less stimulating; for example, reading-- the ringing stayed under more control. If I were concentrating hard on listening and trying to filter out background noise from someone's voice, I would become fatigued, dizzy, and feel like I needed to close my eyes and escape the overstimulation.

While disruptive to anyone, these symptoms were particularly difficult for me because I am a mental health counselor, and I love my career: listening, connecting with human beings, helping them with coping strategies, or looking at situations from different perspectives. The more intently I focused on what an individual was saying, the more exhausted I became. The backbone of my career was based on listening. This exhaustion was all very new. I worked for over twenty years, seeing a full day of clients. My strength of listening and connecting was now becoming a challenge due to the tumor and its location between my ear and my brain. Would I be able to continue being a mental health counselor? Would I have to change careers at this point in my life? Would I be able to work at all?

I specialize in working with children and providing mental health counseling. This requires me to get up and down off the floor many times during an hour-long session. This was never a problem for me until I started having balance issues. Now, I would have to have something to balance or pull myself up to a standing position. If I did not, I often would wobble and sometimes have to steady myself with the wall like I was drunk. Children are very active. One day, a little boy was banging on a toy musical instrument in my office playroom, putting me on the edge of my breaking point. My head was hurting so badly that day I just wanted to sit in a silent room by myself. The session finally ended, and I went home and slept again, my cocoon, my retreat.

The sounds of my day were like city traffic. It started being quiet and manageable in the morning, but after a few hours of intense listening in my office, I needed to escape into the quiet stillness of sleep. My brain was becoming overwhelmed, trying to filter out the noise in my head to hear the person talking to me. I needed to push the mute button, but life kept coming at me. Maybe working full-time in my therapy office would have to change. What variables would I be able to maneuver to promote health and healing?

After working, I would have to sleep for one to two hours each day before I could function at night at home. Luckily, most days, my oldest son (age sixteen) could drive his younger brothers to their activities, or extended family would help while my husband was still at work. My sons and husband also made many evening meals for the family if I was sleeping. My kids have always been my number one priority, and now I was sleeping excessively when I got off work for the day. I was under pressure to continue to pay the bills at my new office building, so work had to be a priority, but I also wanted to be there for my kids. My husband owns his business as well, and it has many expenses. So, I needed to be financially successful to keep my business afloat. My problem was that there was no longer enough energy to do both and make work and family run smoothly.

Change is hard, especially when it is an unwanted change. When something happens to you, it is much more challenging than if you choose to have an event occur. External locus of control is when you feel like something is happening to you and you do not have control over it. Internal locus of control is when you choose a certain option or path. It is much healthier and easier to accept change when it is something you want and feel like you have control over.

In my therapy practice, I was seeing a young child who was preoccupied with death and dying at a young age. She would cry at night and have difficulty going to sleep, worried that she was going to die. She was not ill and lived a safe lifestyle. I went through targeting her thoughts and helped her understand that she had many facts on her side to live a long and healthy life. Would the same be true for me? Some of the treatment goals for others really hit home for me as well during this trying time.

I saw another client who had a different type of medical issue with the brain, a Chiari malformation. This client also had to have brain surgery and was able to talk about the anxiety and intense feelings regarding the journey.

I was a sounding board and encourager for many people who were going through hardships in their lives. I wanted to model being courageous, making it through this hardship, and managing anxiety. I am not saying that I was not scared. But I could be scared and courageous at the same time. It was not either/or; it was and/both. This was a different way of thinking that was helpful to me.

Could something about this hardship help me improve and grow as a person? Was this even a possibility? We would find out as the story unfolds.

I felt like I was in the prime of my life with my career and my new office near my kids' schools, so I could also be there for them. After finishing college and graduate school, working, and having three sons, it all came together reasonably well. I was content with life, myself, my husband, my children, travel, and extended family being nearby, and then BAM! *I really have a brain tumor. You must be kidding me!* When I told the first couple of people about the diagnosis, I laughed as I told them. I could not believe that this was happening to me. It took me a few months to accept that this was my new reality.

I started individual therapy for myself, and one day, I jokingly told them that I figured it was time to come in for my own therapy because I was telling the frozen meal delivery man and grocery store cashiers that I had recently been diagnosed with a brain tumor. I realized it was important to take some time to process all the intense thoughts and feelings I was having; it was overwhelming. The more I talked about the diagnosis, the easier it was to accept that this was my new reality. My feelings jumped back and forth from shock, humor, disbelief, sadness, anger, and finally, acceptance of my new reality.

How to approach difficult news:

1. Get the facts about your health condition.

2. Express your feelings.

3. Set up a support network.

4. Focus on healthy habits.

5. Set realistic goals.

6. Concentrate on what brings you meaning and purpose.

7. Focus on your abilities, not your limitations.

8. Use various coping strategies.

I faced many complicated feelings about the acoustic neuroma diagnosis. I was angry and shocked that this was happening to me. I had always felt that I was fairly healthy. Looking back, I'd developed a number of strange illnesses throughout the years. I was allergic to many animals and substances, like grass, sunflowers, mold, and dust. When I was around five, my parents got my sister and me a family dog for Christmas. The dog slept in our room on Christmas Eve, and I was extremely sick and had trouble breathing. The next day, I was hospitalized and put in an oxygen tent. I remember the clear plastic tent around my hospital bed and looking out at my family members with the oxygen being pumped in through a large tube.

I also had food allergies that other people in my family did not have. I had an ulcer in high school. On vacation only a few summers ago, I was hospitalized in Colorado and had my gall bladder removed during an emergency surgery. I seemed to have odd things happen to me. My sister called me the "bubble child" when we were kids. My sister loved and wanted to get horses as a kid, but this dream was blocked because I was severely allergic to horses.

I was sad that my life was going to change in uncertain ways. I had anxiety about the unknown and whether I would have facial paralysis, cognitive issues, or sensory issues that may affect my specialized career. There were many unknowns; we would just have to ride the wave and see how it all turned out.

Ride the Wave

I also started thinking about my mortality. I was going to die at some point, and I did not want to die so soon. I wanted to see my children grow up. I also knew that I would not die from the surgery, but life may look completely different post-surgery.

It was hard for me to be patient. I like to educate myself on an issue, decide, and then move forward. This acoustic neuroma would be a multi-step process to research options, set up surgery, and rehabilitation. The rehabilitation had many unknowns. *How long would it take? Would I return to my functioning self?* I am patient with others but have never been that patient with myself. This was going to take some work and learning to talk to myself differently.

Have patience with all things, but, first of all with yourself.

Saint Francis De Sales

How long would it take to climb this mountain? Would I make it? What is the best decision at the crossroads? What is it going to take to reach the other side?

I remember the day clearly. I was at an appointment and decided that I needed to accept the brain tumor diagnosis for what it was. I needed to make the most educated choice on how to progress with my treatment. If I left the tumor untreated, I would most likely lose all the hearing on one side, which is called single-sided deafness. I did not want to feel dizzy and have trouble balancing any longer. I decided to enter into the ring of fire. I would hopefully come out on the other side, ready for the second half of my life to begin.

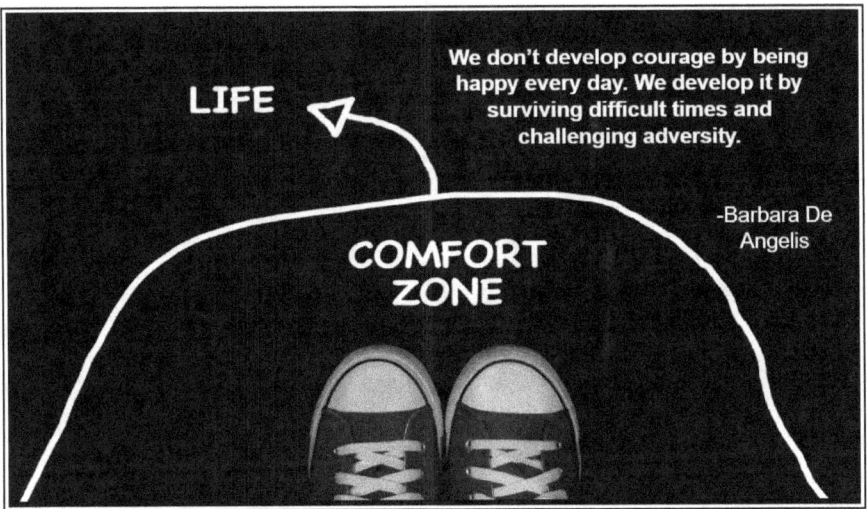

Have you ever gone through a difficult experience where you were forced to make the best choice out of two not-so-good choices? How did you handle the decision-making process? What were the most important factors for you in your stressful time? How did you come to a decision?

CHAPTER 3

Facts about an Acoustic Neuroma

learned to appreciate my husband in a new way with the diagnosis of the brain tumor. He stayed up late researching acoustic neuroma, the treatment of an acoustic neuroma, and recommendations on treatment hospitals and surgeons. I often went to bed early because I was exhausted by my symptoms, and he would take our baton and run with it. He would send me articles and videos from doctors with information and professional opinions of different situations.

After discovering the acoustic neuroma, we were told we would need to research and get professional opinions. I was surprised we were not directed exactly what to do, why, and where. Many variables affect whether people choose to have surgery or not. We needed to see the whole picture to make our decision. We needed to see the forest through the trees. If I did not have surgery, would the symptoms stay the same or get worse? Was there any chance that they might subside? If I chose to have the surgery, would my quality of life get even worse? Would it be worse for the first year and then I would bounce back?

The first step was to learn about acoustic neuromas to have the knowledge to make an educated treatment decision. This information is from the University of California San Diego, Head and Neck (Otolaryngology Department).

What is an acoustic neuroma?

An acoustic neuroma is a rare tumor. It is not cancerous. It grows slowly from an overproduction of Schwann cells that coat the vestibular nerve and is also called a vestibular schwannoma. The tumor then presses on the hearing and balance nerves in the inner ear, creating undesirable symptoms. Schwann cells typically wrap around and support nerve fibers. A large tumor can press on the facial nerve, which controls facial muscles and sensation. Depending on size and location, it can press on other brain structures.

There are two types of acoustic neuromas:

- Unilateral acoustic neuromas. This type affects only one ear. It is the most common type of acoustic neuroma. This tumor may develop at any age. It most often happens between ages thirty and sixty. Acoustic neuroma may be the result of nerve damage caused by environmental factors. The only certain environmental risk factor is past radiation to the head. It is unclear if prolonged exposure to loud noises is a cause of acoustic neuromas.

- Bilateral acoustic neuromas. This type affects both ears and is inherited. It is caused by a genetic problem called neurofibromatosis-2 (NF2).

What causes an acoustic neuroma?

Acoustic neuroma can be caused by:

- Failure of a governor gene to suppress the growth of Schwann cells—those cells responsible for coating the nerve fibers with insulation.

- Neck or head radiation. This can lead to acoustic neuroma many years later.

- Neurofibromatosis type 2 (NF2). People with this disease are at higher risk. NF2 can run in families.

- Unknown etiologies

What are the symptoms of an acoustic neuroma?

These are the most common symptoms of acoustic neuroma:

- Hearing loss on one side, cannot hear high-frequency sounds

- A feeling of fullness in the ear

- A ringing in the ear (tinnitus) on the side of the tumor

- Dizziness

- Balance problems or unsteadiness

- Headaches, a clumsy walk, and mental confusion

The symptoms of acoustic neuroma may look like other conditions or health problems. Always talk with your healthcare provider for a diagnosis.

How is an acoustic neuroma diagnosed?

Acoustic neuromas look like other middle and inner ear problems. They may be hard to diagnose. An ear exam and a hearing test are often done first. A CT scan and MRI can help to find and measure the tumor.

How is an acoustic neuroma treated?

Treatment will depend on your symptoms, age, and general health. It will also depend on the severity of the condition.

Treatment may include watching and waiting, surgery, or radiation. Surgery for larger tumors can damage hearing, balance, and facial nerves. Another treatment choice is radiosurgery, such as Gamma Knife®. This uses focused radiation to reduce the size or blunt the growth of the tumor.

What are the complications of an acoustic neuroma?

The tumor can press against the brain stem if it gets big enough. This can affect neurological function or even become life-threatening.

Be aware that this is not medical advice. I am not a doctor, and treatment options advance and change often. This is basic information about an acoustic neuroma from UC San Diego Health, an article on Acoustic Neuroma by Dr. Ashutosh Kacker et al.

We started collecting data and decided which treatment hospitals were closest and their specialization with brain surgery. We created a list of questions to ask each medical team regarding their medical opinion on my acoustic neuroma, what treatment they would recommend if surgery was recommended, what type of surgery, how many of these procedures they had completed, and the outcomes.

We would drive to Denver for the first medical opinion. The three other hospitals provided telehealth evaluations, which was a blessing. We had a plan and were on our way to solving this dilemma.

CHAPTER 4

Learning from Others

After many weeks of researching acoustic neuromas, we were starting to understand better what this tumor was and how to proceed. We read repeatedly to get expert opinions from many different medical teams. Variables are vastly different for everyone with these types of tumors. Variables that can help determine surgery, radiation, or watch and wait are:

- the location of the tumor on the nerve and within the brain

- the size of the tumor and rate of change

- your age and general health

- your resilience with past surgeries

Being connected to others with acoustic neuromas

I became connected with others who had been diagnosed with acoustic neuromas through social media (private groups) and by word of mouth with friends of a friend. My husband and I had a phone call one evening with a woman in our town. She was diagnosed with an acoustic neuroma several years earlier and had it surgically removed in California at a medical facility called The House Clinic in Los Angeles. She explained that she was doing relatively well. She was now retired from her teaching career but seemed to recuperate well. She spoke about how it is harder to balance when walking in the dark, but she had adapted.

I started interacting with other individuals around the world who have been diagnosed with acoustic neuroma via social media. I received a message from a woman in Sweden explaining that with socialized medicine, she could not get the surgery she needed. She explained that she was facing daily struggles from the tumor but that her doctor did not recommend surgery yet, so the federal insurance would not pay for her craniotomy. She was inquiring how much surgery costs in America to see if she could afford to pay for it on her own. I shared with her the cost as I understood it from my perspective as an American citizen. She did not respond for quite a long time over text. My heart went out to her and her situation.

She and I were in the same boat, being diagnosed with the same kind of brain tumor. However, due to her country having socialized medicine, she was not in control of whether she could get the surgery. This made me realize that even though I had been diagnosed with a brain tumor (which I still had a tough time accepting), at least I had good insurance that would help pay for the expensive, extremely complicated procedure if this were the route I decided to take.

Some of the people that I connected with who had recovered from acoustic neuroma surgery seemed to be doing well and had most of their daily lives back. People were reporting running, hiking, being able to get back to work, and spending time with family and friends without issues.

However, others who had this surgery were having tremendous struggles. They were not able to get back to their careers or driving. They had to sleep much more than others because their brains were being overstimulated. Some were receiving disability because they could no longer work. The people more vocal in the group were suffering the most, the people whose issues had not resolved after surgery. I tried to take this into consideration, but it was frightening to think that my life may be forever changed by surgery.

Communicating and learning from others who were more knowledgeable on the topic was key. I had never heard of this type of tumor before being diagnosed, but now I was starting to feel familiar with the research, vocabulary, and options available.

From the research, we learned that this is not a one-size-fits-all approach. We met with four different medical teams that treat acoustic neuromas. Having as much information as possible was important to be thorough before deciding how to treat the tumor.

Four Medical Opinions

One of the most prestigious medical teams, the Mayo Clinic, endorsed the watch-and-wait approach. They said that removing the tumor may create more symptomology and dysfunction than leaving the small tumor in my head. They were leaning towards the watch-and-wait approach. However, they thought the middle cranial fossa approach would be selected if surgery were done.

Another team, the one closest to where we live geographically (Denver), agreed that having surgery was the best decision (due to my symptoms). The middle cranial fossa approach was the type of surgery I needed, but they did not do a large number of these surgeries. They were very willing to do the surgery, but my husband and I were uncomfortable with the small number of middle cranial fossa surgeries they had done at that hospital. We decided that surgery made sense, but we needed to find a medical team that did most of the middle cranial fossa.

We were extremely impressed by the surgeon from the third team at the University of Utah, but he also had not done many middle cranial fossa approaches on a very regular basis. He agreed that having it surgically removed was my best option and gave me hope that the ringing could stop down the road on the left side of my head since the ringing may have started due to Covid. We discovered later that he was accurate in his assessment. My left ear did stop ringing one evening in January of 2023, a year after it had begun. I was sitting at my kitchen table on a dark winter night and suddenly had clarity in my left ear. I shouted this out to my family members. "My left ear stopped ringing!"

I was ecstatic! The unwelcome news from the surgeon in Utah was after the brain surgery, the right ear (with the tumor) would continue to ring as that symptom would not be relieved with surgery, and he was accurate about that as well. So I went from just the left ear ringing to surgery, where they both rang for several months, and then the left stopped twelve months after it started with the Covid diagnosis.

The fourth team, the University of California, San Diego, was eager to take out the tumor, explaining that I "would never be younger and the tumor would never be smaller." This made sense to us. Just having the tumor in your skull could create one-sided deafness at any time. Keeping the tumor in seemed like playing Russian roulette. Also, if the tumor became too large, it could press on the brainstem, creating increased problems and possibly death.

The Deciding Moment

The moment that helped me decide to schedule the surgery was on a warm spring evening when my middle son and I went to the grocery store to pick up just a few items after a baseball game. While shopping in the meat aisle, I went on total sensory overload. I had to stop and hold onto the meat counter coolers to avoid falling. My son did not know what was going on and why I stopped walking. I explained to him how dizzy I was and that I needed to stop momentarily and regain my balance. He looked scared, and we both felt frightened. Could I not even go to the grocery store with my son to pick up a few items?

Soon after, I decided to schedule the craniotomy to remove my acoustic neuroma.

I am a mother, a wife, a daughter, a sister, a friend, and a licensed mental health therapist. When I was diagnosed with my brain tumor, I was running the race of life at a pretty fast pace. The acoustic neuroma was slowing me down tremendously due to not feeling well. I was experiencing headaches, pressure in my ear (which we thought were ear infections), feeling overstimulated by noise and too much interaction, sensory overload, ringing in my ears that became louder the longer I was awake, balance issues, hearing loss, and dizziness (an ongoing carsick feeling or feeling like my head was bobbing in a fish bowl).

We contacted the University of California San Diego and scheduled my middle cranial fossa brain surgery for August 16, 2022.

If you are trying to decide on how to move forward with treatment, this is a very complex decision. If I were less symptomatic, I would have chosen the watch-and-wait route. Often, these tumors grow very slowly or not at all. Many people choose to have their tumors stay intact and have them monitored for growth each year.

For individuals who have more difficulty recovering or who do not recover, there is still hope in viewing life differently. It is hard when you are in pain or nauseous to have a positive mindset, but it is better than the alternative. You will not have a positive mindset some days, period. Some days are just horrible, and there are no other words for it. Hopefully, those days can become few and far between.

It is hopeful and helpful to talk to others who are in your shoes or have already walked the path of this decision-making, treatment, and recovery/rehabilitation. A sense of community and connection is of utmost importance because these are rare tumors and not well understood by the general public.

I felt hopeful and ready to move forward after scheduling the surgery. I also felt terrified of brain surgery and wanted to run away from the problem. Unfortunately, running away was not an option.

My father asked me to write the next chapter, which was an excellent idea. How can you support your loved one in traveling through this journey of living with an acoustic neuroma? What can I say or do, and more importantly, what should I not say that might make them feel worse?

CHAPTER 5

How Can You Support Your Loved One?

What a person with an acoustic neuroma wants others to know:

1. Know that it is very frightening.

When I started reading about acoustic neuroma, it appeared that it would not be that bad. The tumor is not cancerous and most likely will not kill you if it is monitored. However, you may have dizziness, tinnitus, headaches, and ear pain that cannot be treated very well. In my case, I had to slow down substantially, work less in my professional career, and interact less with family and friends. I felt overstimulated much of the time and was exhausted.

2. It is often not obvious what is the best treatment, and the experts frequently disagree.

After talking to my first two medical teams, I decided it would be best to leave the tumor alone and just monitor it with MRIs. Then, I started experiencing more symptoms, which made it hard to function. I was feeling ill for more days than not and life became very unpredictable. After talking with the next two medical teams and my symptoms were bothering me almost every day, I reconsidered getting the surgery sooner rather than later. The medical teams give recommendations, but these opinions are often different. As the patient, you have to evaluate and choose unless it has grown so big that it is life-threatening.

3. The two items above create uncertainty.
4. It is a huge decision to feel uncertain about.

Could my symptoms lessen or are they going to increase? Can I tolerate this for my quality of life from here forward?

5. Symptoms vary day by day and hour by hour.
6. This can be frustrating after feeling well for a period of time and then feeling dizzy and nauseous again and not knowing why.
7. In the morning, I often felt fine.

The longer the day went, the more disoriented I felt. People with ANs call this "wonky head." It is hard to plan and honor commitments.

8. If I was invited to an event, I never knew if I would feel up to it when the moment arrived.

I like to be dependable, but I would often cancel if not feeling well the day of an event.

9. **The symptoms can make simple tasks difficult and exhausting.**

Headaches, tinnitus, facial twitches, and jaw pain were common for me before surgery. Going to sleep felt like the best option.

10. **The symptoms can make conversations and socializing difficult.**

It is hard to be attentive when talking with people when you just want to close your eyes and retreat to a quiet and dark place.

11. **The distraction of tinnitus and/or dizziness can slow the processing of speech, attention, and memory.**
12. **I would forget what I was doing or saying more often than other people my age.**

"We found this in your brain."

(Reprint permission granted, CartoonStock)

13. Mobility can be affected greatly.

This includes balance, walking in the dark, taking stairs, walking close to other people and bumping into them, difficulty walking and turning my head simultaneously. Post-surgery, I could not walk on my own.

The gait belt was needed to help me retrain myself to walk and keep my balance. While walking, I had great difficulty turning my head to look and see if a car was coming to cross the street. I would have to stop and then turn my head to stay stable. I remember walking in a parking garage in California, and I could not identify where the sounds were coming from or if a car was approaching. It was difficult to look back and forth for the approaching car, and I just wanted to put my hands over my ears and close my eyes to block out the stimulation. This, of course, would have been very dangerous. I grabbed ahold of my husband or one of my sons, and it probably looked like I was having a panic attack. Anxiety engulfed my body during these moments.

Also, later in my recovery, when I was walking around my neighborhood, I could not turn my head to say hi to someone without veering or getting off balance. I would look straight ahead, which felt very strange and antisocial for both parties in the situation. This goes to show that you never know what someone is going through and give them the benefit of the doubt that they are not trying to be rude.

14. Facial paralysis can make a person feel very self-conscious.

I, fortunately, did not have facial paralysis, but this can be very difficult and heartbreaking for people who end up with this condition temporarily or permanently. People will stare and try to see what is going on with the person with the AN. It can hurt self-confidence significantly when a person's facial tone is asymmetric.

"If you see someone without a smile, give them one of yours."

-Dolly Parton

15. Benign does not mean the tumor will be a walk in the park.

It is in the brain. Brain surgery is major surgery with a very LONG recovery. In my mind, a couple of months is a long recovery. I learned to think differently about what a long recovery entails. After this type of brain surgery, you have recovery in the first year and into the second year.

It is positive that the tumor is benign, but it is going to be an uphill battle getting it out of this area.

I did feel happy that the tumor was benign. But it was not like having a mole removed. It was going to be a life-changing benign tumor.

16. The time it takes to recover is much longer than normal surgery or illness.

I was told this many times. But I was ready to feel better right away. I would feel better and then feel worse repeatedly. I was often afraid to say I was doing better because soon after, I would take a turn for the worse again. It was hard to keep saying that I was feeling worse again because it made me feel depressed and like a hypochondriac. I knew others were hoping that I was feeling better as well. I just started to grin and bear it.

Be patient. Even if it looks like they are doing great, they are often not. Do not expect them to keep up on normal tasks just because they *look fine.*

I was excited and pleased when people told me I looked great my first week out from surgery. But soon, I wanted to yell, "I look fine, but I sure do not feel fine." Looks can be deceiving.

17. Please invite them to smaller gatherings or restaurants with less noise and people.

Hearing people in large, overwhelming environments is hard, and sensory issues may overload them. Learn about acoustic neuromas and ask how your acoustic neuroma person is doing.

18. **Ask about their symptoms that day and what would be helpful.**

Or, if it looks like the person is tired of talking about this roller coaster of feeling good and then feeling bad again, find a mutual topic of interest to share with one another. Sometimes, the person is tired of talking about the AN and the trouble it is causing.

19. **A person with an acoustic neuroma may not be able to do something today that they did fine yesterday, which can be very confusing to family and friends.**

If you are able to go out to eat one night then why are you sleeping most of the next day? That was the way it went for the first year. I had difficulty finding a pattern of what was wearing me out, except if I got a cold or felt sick. Then, it put me down, sleeping for days. Horrible. It was a nightmare for a person who thrived on being productive.

Destroy the idea that you have to be constantly working or grinding in order to be successful. Embrace the concept that rest, recovery. And reflection are essential parts of the progress toward a successful and ultimately happy life.

-Author Unknown

20. Help them with family obligations and responsibilities.

Have other family members step up to do the grocery shopping or make meals. It just became the norm for other people to handle these responsibilities, especially after a day at my office. Simple directions or preparation was much easier than multiple steps for recipes and meals.

21. If the acoustic neuroma person asks you to repeat what you said, please repeat it and do not look annoyed.

I think this may be the hardest for teenage offspring. They would mumble something, and I would ask them to repeat it. Sometimes they would, and other times they would not, depending on their mood.

22. Be forgiving and understanding about brain fog.

I became very frustrated with myself when I was trying to do executive functioning tasks such as remembering a list, paying attention, or managing my time. I also saw frustration on the faces of others when I forgot bits of information frequently.

I would try to bring something from work home or from home to work, and it would take many tries to succeed. This was very frustrating to me. I like to be productive and not feel like I am chasing my tail.

23. Do not tell the person with the acoustic neuroma that it could be worse.

This goes for almost any medical issue or life stressor. The person needs to feel that you understand their point of view, where they are coming from, and that you care. At some point, they will come to terms with the idea, "it could be worse," but on their OWN time. That is not for you to say to them if you are trying to be understanding and be empathic. It is better not to say anything at all if this thought comes to mind to share. I had many well-meaning people say this to me after I had my two miscarriages. If there is one great takeaway from reading this book, I would highlight the above suggestion.

Empathy is the ability to understand and care about what someone is going through. When you feel someone really cares, it can be very healing. The person does not feel as alone and that they feel supported.

CHAPTER 6

A Higher Power

elieving in a higher power helped me to feel less anxious about the tumor. I have always been a religious person, praying and feeling that there is a higher power that takes care of every one of us. I was not sure why I was chosen to have this tumor in my brain, and at first, I was sad and angry about it. I was able to work through this over time and then felt comfort knowing that I could pray about all my worries and that there was a higher power watching over me.

It is hard when something terrible happens, and a person may wonder if God is punishing them. Why is this happening to me? What is the purpose of this happening to me? I had experienced two miscarriages in my thirties, and these were two other times when my faith weakened for a while. I did not understand why this would happen to a family that was yearning for a baby and was preparing a loving home for the baby's arrival. This took me a while to get through, finally coming to terms with the fact that something was not forming physically in my body with the fetus and that I had to become strong and let go of what I could not control. I could not control that acoustic neuroma. I could not control that it was growing in my skull or the rate at which it would grow. I did have the choice to get it removed. These medical traumas were opposite in a way. I wanted to keep the babies and grow them as much as possible. They were taken from me. I did not want the brain tumor, and there it was growing without my permission.

Can you relate to this experience when something exceedingly difficult happened in your life, and you wondered why?

The miscarriages were similar to the acoustic neuroma because I could not control growth or death, and it was all taking place inside my body. It did not make logical sense, but it was not up to me. These were forces that I could not control, no matter how hard I tried.

I tried to remember that I had gotten through tough times before and could get through more hard times. This was a genetic abnormality, just as the miscarriages were abnormalities as well. In psychology, we talk about nature and nurture. There are biological issues that we face with our human bodies, as well as environmental issues.

I started seeing God as the power that would help me through this traumatic time rather than the one to blame for this nightmare.

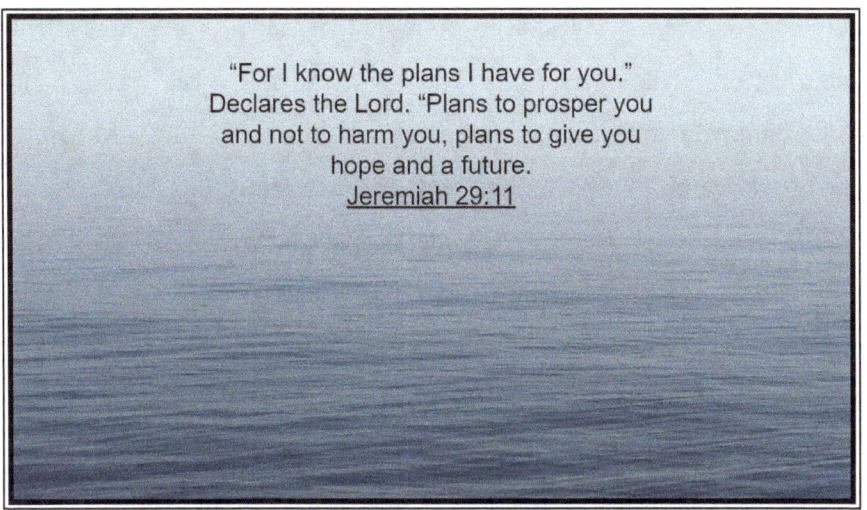

"For I know the plans I have for you."
Declares the Lord. "Plans to prosper you
and not to harm you, plans to give you
hope and a future.
Jeremiah 29:11

Our congregation has a church bulletin that includes announcements and a list of people in need of prayers. My husband is very private, and he hesitated about having my name put in the church bulletin for people needing prayers. I saw the issue entirely differently. The more people prayed for me, the better my outcome. People deal with hard experiences differently. I feel that having people caring and praying for me really did help my positive outcome with the surgery. I believe in the power of prayer and all the positive energy of others surrounding you.

I feel like my faith and spiritual life grew stronger after this hardship. It helped me focus on what is really important in life and why. I thank my friends and family for the prayers and positive energy sent my way during this time. I try to have positive energy, direct it towards others, and pray for those struggling.

What are your thoughts on a higher power? Do you feel that events happen for a reason in the world?

The stained glass windows in our church let the light through in many different ways.

CHAPTER 7

Preparing for My Leave of Absence

At work, I would completely focus on my clients and engage and be present regarding their issues and goals. It was nice to throw myself into work and focus on clients instead of thinking about my issues. Therapists are trained to keep personal issues to themselves to be neutral sounding boards for their clients. That is how we are trained in graduate school. The session is for the client. If clients become worried or too concerned about their therapist, they may not focus and work on their own goals. This is natural and expected. After all, it is a relationship. However, the client needs to trust that the therapist can be a container to hold and manage tough feelings, memories, and situations so the client can talk freely about the issues causing them difficulty.

This became an odd experience for me professionally. Once the surgery was approaching, I had to prepare clients and let children and families know that I would be gone on medical leave for a couple of months.

Therapists do not usually talk about themselves or what is going on in their lives, but this was an exception. Clients would, of course, inquire about what was going on, and they were then concerned about me and if I would be all right. For adult clients, I would explain what was going on, that it was a benign tumor, and that it would be removed, making it sound as routine as possible. When talking to my child clients, I would explain that the doctors knew how to fix what was going on, and they would remove a part that was making me feel sick through surgery, and then I would recover. Some of my adolescent clients surprised me the most because they are naturally egocentric and think that things happen in the world because of them. I had one adolescent client I had been meeting with a long term who was worried about this surgery. I had been one of the few consistent figures in their life, and they had gone through many emotional events. Initially, therapy was court-ordered, but even after they no longer had to attend therapy, they continued therapy on their own. I explained to them that I would be okay and that I would be back to meet with them again after my medical leave. When I returned to work, they were among the first clients I met over the computer for telehealth sessions from my home.

My clients had also noticed how often I was canceling sessions, which was very unlike me. In the past, like all professionals, occasionally I would have a sick day, but in the year leading up to surgery, I had repeated ear infections and canceled sessions more often. Staying in bed with my eyes closed was the best way to handle these symptoms. Then, I felt like I was back to normal until another ear infection would pop up. I was often prescribed medication to clear up the ear infections. Then, I felt like I was back to normal until another ear infection popped up. During the height of the Covid pandemic, I called my primary care clinic, and a doctor came out to my car to check my ears and throat through my opened window, diagnosing me with another ear infection. I got back on medication, and it felt like it cleared up again for a while. I thought it was odd that I was getting reoccurring ear infections but had no idea that it would be the first symptom of my brain tumor.

Resilience

CHAPTER 8

How Confronting Challenges Leads to Healing

felt relieved that I had decided to have my acoustic neuroma surgically removed and to move forward. I had been going back and forth for a couple of months regarding the pros and cons of leaving the tumor in (in case it was growing slowly) or taking it out now and getting the whole thing over with.

On good days, I would feel content with leaving the tumor in and going with the conservative approach of monitoring the growth. On harder days, I was so frustrated knowing I did not want to live such a lower quality of life, sleeping often to escape my vestibular symptoms in my skull.

My mind continued to go back to *not wanting* to have to deal with the tumor when my family was in other important phases of life. My sons were growing up quickly and would soon be doing college campus tours; we still had vacations to go on, and my sons might get married or have kids in the next ten years. I did not want to have to worry about the tumor needing to be removed at some unknown time in the future. I started experiencing more symptoms and felt tired and overwhelmed most days. I needed much more sleep, but at the same time, I could not sleep well at night due to my anxiety about the tumor.

I am an advocate of the idea of doing the worst part of a task first to get it over with so the rest of the task will be easier. I felt relief when I thought about eating the frog and getting this surgery done and over with before I got any older.

If it's your job to eat a frog, it's best to do it first thing in the morning. And if it's your job to eat two frogs, it's best to eat the biggest one first.

-Mark Twain

My husband is intelligent, organized, and reliable. He was the one who took charge of the research, scheduled the surgery, dealt with insurance, and made reservations. He made reservations for us at a hospital housing apartment complex, La Jolla Family House, on the university campus. This apartment was phenomenal because it was a fraction of the price of the hotels in the affluent La Jolla area in California. The staff and other residents understood the situation we were in. It was also right on the campus, so it was a short walk to the hospital.

I am from a very close-knit family, and my parents and sister proposed that we would take a week-long vacation out in San Diego, on the beach, before my surgery date. I have always loved the beach and find it the most relaxing place in the world. My parents, sister, and her husband paid for our accommodation in the beach condo. Finances were getting a little stressful at this point, and they offered to pay for our room and board for the beach vacation, and I did not argue. They had hearts of gold to do this for us. Two of my boys would be going along to California with us, and my oldest decided to stay home for his high school soccer season that was underway. I also wanted him to be with us, but I also understood that it was important to him to stay in his routine and not be gone for two weeks when his soccer season had just begun.

The plan was set; ready or not, here we come! But first, we would plan a big party with friends and family to say goodbye before taking off on this journey.

CHAPTER 9

One Last Hurrah with Friends and Family

I have always been very sociable and have thrown many parties in the past. During Covid, we did not have any parties but were looking forward to being festive once again when Covid was at bay. We decided to have a big party before we left for California. My sister was gracious enough to host this at her house because the party room at a restaurant in town that I was trying to arrange was already booked.

We invited friends and family. I have always been an *over-inviter* because the more, the merrier. I do not like people feeling left out of a social event. I had my closest friends attend the event, neighbors, acquaintances, aunts and uncles, my kids' friends, and sports friends. It was a great party. Overstimulation was hard for me at this point, but I felt that it would be worth it to have one more big party before the surgery. I have had many theme parties in the past, including Cinco de Mayo, Halloween, and backyard fall parties with changing leaves around the fire table on the back deck, but the one still on my bucket list was a Roaring Twenties party. I was excited for people to dress up like flappers and gangsters and spend the evening socializing and having fun. We had a huge cake, lots of beads, fancy hats, speakeasy drinks, appetizers brought in by friends, and lots of conversation, catching up, and laughter. I felt honored and happy, sad, proud, nervous, and grateful seeing all the friends and family who took the time to attend my party. We were all connected like a necklace of beads coming together to create something strong and unified.

The party signified the beginning of a new chapter in life. I was excited and relieved that I had decided to have the surgery, but I also knew that this might be the last big sensory, social event for me. I did not know if these kinds of parties would suit me well once I had the brain surgery. Men wore fedoras and bowler hats, while women sported sequin headbands for flare and style. My flapper headband would soon be traded for a wrap of white gauze.

PART 2

CHAPTER 10

To California, We Go

I was excited about the beach vacation lined up in the condominium between Pacific Beach and Mission Beach. We had a condominium rented on Ocean Front Walk. It was the perfect setting for the beach lover.

What a blessing it was to have such supportive people in my life coming to California and trying to enjoy a family vacation leading up to this life-changing event. I have always been close to my sister. She is three years older than I and chose not to have children of her own. She is like my three sons' second mother and often helps us. She lives close by and is always ready to help give a kid a ride to practice, bring them food, or simply spend time with one or all three of my boys. My parents have also been so supportive, and I am blessed that God gave me to this couple to raise me and be in my life each day. The week in California, spending time at the beach was wonderful. We also went to a San Diego Padres game, which my sons thoroughly enjoyed. What a great family that had my back at this challenging time in life.

My husband did not choose to go for the beach vacation. He was worried about money and taking so much time off work. We are both self-employed, which makes medical hardships very difficult. We did not have any sick days or days for medical leave. My husband chose to stay home with our oldest son and continue to work during the beach vacation. Then, he would fly out to California and be with me and the rest of the family before we moved from the beach to the hospital/campus apartment housing. Since we are both self-employed, we have always had to buy health insurance out of pocket instead of having it supplied by our employer. The premiums go up yearly, and currently, we pay about US$2000 a month for health insurance for a family of five. This is the first year I was not frustrated paying the monthly premium because I was grateful we had good insurance to cover most of this surgery.

My husband Eric flew in the night before we moved to the hospital/campus housing. The day he flew in, I started feeling anxious and a little sick to my stomach, knowing that this was going to have to happen. I may have canceled the surgery if it were solely up to me. But I knew I needed to get it over with and move forward in life. Once Eric was in California, I joked with him about how I was going to run away so he could not take me to the hospital. He said he would run after me. Yes, I needed to have this surgery.

I had just finished crying before this picture. We were leaving the beach house and moving to the hospital/campus apartments. I wiped the tears away and smiled.

I was hoping and praying that I would recover fully and have my life back to normal in the next year. I felt like I had a lot of good years left in me.

CHAPTER 11

One Day Until Surgery

A rrangements were made for my parents to stay nearby in a hotel, and my sister and brother-in-law flew back home to be with my oldest son. When we arrived at hospital/campus housing, the employee checking us in had us all sit at a table to complete forms. She asked who the patient was and for what procedure. I started to feel as if I were going to cry at this point, but I was holding back tears because my two younger sons were at the table with us. I did not want them to think this surgery would not turn out okay. I have always told my boys that it is okay to feel all feelings, but I was trying to hold myself together so they could follow my lead. I did not want to burden my kids with adult problems, but these had been thrown in the lap of everyone. I wanted the boys to know that being together and supporting each other through hard times was of utmost importance. But I certainly did not want to burden them with thinking they had to take care of their mother emotionally. What a hard spot it was to be in that afternoon around the round table in the housing building common room. I did some deep breathing and pulled myself together. The woman then asked me what building I would be in for the surgery, and I did not know.

I knew I would be with Dr. Friedman and Dr. Schwartz at the University of California-San Diego Hospital. Tears started running down my face, and Eric was able to answer the questions for her. *How was I going to make it through this surgery if I did not even know where I was going?* I started to speak harshly to myself, which did not help. I disengaged by tuning out and letting others take control. She explained that the medical building where my procedure would take place was only a short walk across a footbridge. *A short walk, we could do that. This would be achievable.* We would later walk across the footbridge that would open up the new world that would consume us for the next few days. When I was stable enough to leave the hospital, we would return to the campus/hospital apartment housing. One step at a time over the bridge to this life-changing adventure.

We had to wear masks in the communal areas of the campus apartment. I was pro mask at this point with Covid, but since I was having so much anxiety anyway, this made it hard for me to breathe. I had to focus on taking long, deep breaths because my breathing had become shallow due to anxiety. The campus housing had a grounding technique poster to help people reduce anxiety by naming something they can see, hear, touch, taste, and smell. This helps bring people back into the here and now and to stop the anxious thoughts from running wild in one's head. After seeing the sign, it also reminded me that all these feelings surging through me were normal and that other patients were experiencing this, too. That is why the sign was placed on the front desk. *Breathe, everything will be okay.*

La Jolla Family House Apartments

> **"**
> *If you can't fly then run, if you can't run then walk, if you can't walk then crawl, but whatever you do you have to keep moving forward.*
> **"**
>
> ### Martin Luther King Jr.

We had pre-operation appointments the day before surgery and met with the physical therapist. They had me do pre-op physical therapy activities to compare with my physical therapy activities post-op. I was excited that I was able to do most of the activities well. I have never been the most coordinated person, but I was able to walk around the small orange cones in patterns. I had difficulty walking the straight line on the floor, so I knew this would be incredibly difficult for me post-surgery. I also had a lot of blood work done, and my arms were bandaged up.

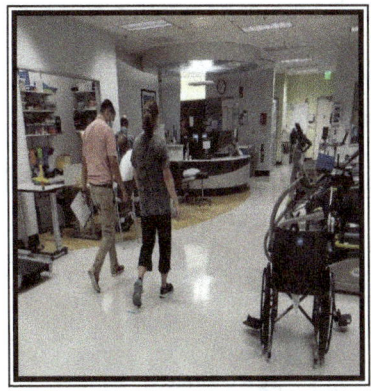
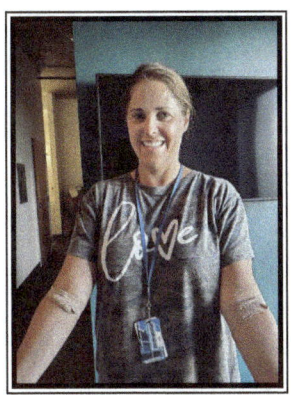

I did not get very much sleep the night before the surgery. But somehow, my husband and I overslept with a glitch alarm on the cell phone. Life was throwing an unexpected curve ball in there again! Instead of getting angry about oversleeping, we just rolled with the punches and made it work to the best of our ability, a common theme in our life recently. My dad was there early to pick us up from the apartment to drop us off at the hospital's front doors, as it was still dark out because it was so early. I would have several hours that would be missing from my day during the surgery. Time would not run as usual. I would miss this day's most important hours, thankfully being under anesthesia.

My sons continued to sleep at the campus apartment, and the surgery would begin very soon. I was grateful that we could stay in the campus family housing. It reminded me of the apartment I shared in college with my college roommates. How different times were now, with us all preparing for this major surgery instead of eating popcorn and watching television laughing with my college roommates.

My parents have been so supportive of me through thick and thin. We reminisced about the campus apartment looking like my college apartment many years ago. It is a funny story. They helped me move my belongings five hours east to go to college. I was supposed to live in a house called the Mudhole. I had paid rent to save my spot in that house all summer, but it was in horrible condition when we arrived. We moved my belongings in because I am strong-willed, but the night before they traveled back home, I told them that I did not want to live there and that *we needed to do something drastic.* The next day, by some miracle, we found an opening at a brand-new college apartment. I would feel safe there; the windows opened, and it had heat. My parents have always been there for me, even when *we have to do something drastic.*

Bob and Jan Arnio (my parents)

My dad has often called me a "heat-seeking missile." If I put my mind to something, I would get it done. This personality trait was helpful to me during this period of my life. I could not give up.

I was grateful for the loved ones who held my hand, drove me to the hospital, and sat at the hospital waiting for me to come out of surgery. I am not sure I could have done this on my own. I am not sure anyone would be able to go through this alone. Thank you to all the people in the world who show up for others when they need a helping hand and someone to lean on.

CHAPTER 12

Transformation

O nce we were at the hospital and went through the check-in procedure, I noticed a beautiful collage of butterfly art on the wall. This really spoke to me. I started thinking of myself as a caterpillar or butterfly that needed to undergo a metamorphosis with this brain surgery. I would be able to emerge into a healthy human being who would no longer have to worry about this annoying tumor. I had also bought a silk scarf with butterflies at our local airport gift shop before getting on the flight to California. I was not sure if I would need a scarf for my head after the surgery because I did not know how much hair they would shave off or cut. The butterfly was a positive image going into the operating room.

This was the moment I felt most alone with my thoughts. I had loved ones near, but I was alone waiting in the pre-operation room. This was it. This process had started, and there was no escape. I had to hold strong. I am a very emotional person, so I "checked out" a bit emotionally. There were too many feelings and I felt like I would burst if I felt them. I had to ignore the feelings for now and keep going.

I had a lot of support throughout this process but now I had to go it alone for a while. Would I be able to keep myself from breaking down? I needed to get a firm grip on my thoughts and not let them run wild. I wanted to avoid the surgery, but that was not going to work. I had to hold strong and get to the other side.

I would wake up about three hours later, opening my eyes very slowly with my loved ones peering over the hospital bed, smiling at me.

CHAPTER 13

The Surgery

The loneliest moment was waiting in a huge university hospital's surgery room.

I was in the room, alone, waiting to be wheeled to the operating room at a large university-based hospital. The nurse who entered the room stated to not put any personal belongings anywhere except the bag provided due to hospital germs. The *hospital germs* sent my anxiety to the next level, thinking about how they were going to open my brain in a place where there were lots of hospital germs. Remember, we had been trying to avoid germs so much over the past two years due to Covid. After getting Covid, my inner ear did not stop ringing. After this ringing, my brain tumor was diagnosed. I was starting a downward spiral in my mind just at the time when I needed to stay as calm as possible. I had to practice deep breathing and working on identifying and changing my thoughts. I had wondered why I had not asked for an anxiety medication to help me before the surgery. Did I just forget to ask, or did I feel I could do anything now? I was not sure, but it was too late now anyway. *It's another curveball that just had to be dealt with; just go with it.* I have had many surgeries in my lifetime, but this one would be the most complicated. I felt cold and tense. I was in a bed with blankets but did not feel relaxed. I started changing the anxious thoughts in my head. I could do this. I have done many hard things in my life, and I could make it through this needed procedure. It was the day and moment I had been waiting for and dreading since the brain tumor diagnosis five months ago.

I started thinking about how my parents probably did not sleep at all the night before the surgery. As a parent, I would not want to see my child go through this. So much depended on the surgical team. What would the outcome be?

I'm sure mistakes happen during surgery, but I had to change the channel of those thoughts in my mind right away. There was nothing productive or helpful coming from those thoughts. It was too late to do anything else to prepare. Now, I just had to wait for this all to begin.

I knew my husband was waiting in the large waiting room of the hospital for skull-based surgeries. My children were with my parents across the bridge at the La Jolla campus apartments. Everyone was waiting for the brain surgery to be complete. I held in my mind that hundreds of friends, relatives, and acquaintances were praying for me and sending positive thoughts and prayers through the miles. I did not want to be there or have this happen, but I knew it needed to be done for me to be able to be tumor-free and continue with my life as normal. I did not choose this tumor, but I did choose to have it removed.

I would wake up after surgery with the brain tumor removed and titanium mesh and a "fat plug" in its place. I was happy to wake up and see my loved ones, but my vision and depth perception had all changed tremendously. Everyone around my bed was blurry. Below is an example of what the world looked like after surgery.

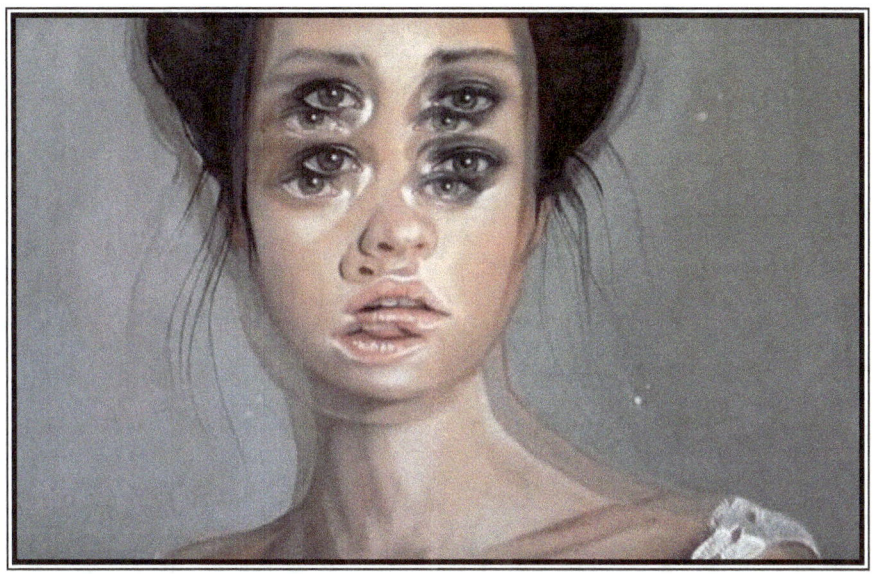

An Example of Vision after surgery (photo shared in Acoustic Neuroma social media group)

I felt nauseous and knew that I looked frightening from the way that my sons and parents were looking at me. When I had a mirror and saw the incision for myself, I could see a large C-shaped incision with twenty-two staples all around above my right ear. The hair around my incision was braided and sticking straight out. I was impressed at how they braided my hair and did not have to shave much hair at all. This was something that I had not asked about with the surgery, but they said they knew how to get it out of the way and not to worry. The UCSD medical team knew exactly what they were doing. I was in good hands. I was thankful we did so much research to be in such a great hospital with a skilled surgical team.

The Surgery Was Complete

The doctors came and told us that the surgery went as planned, and they were able to remove the entire tumor. This was INCREDIBLY positive because the chance of the tumor growing back is reduced if the whole tumor is removed. Sometimes, a sliver of the tumor may be left in because it is wrapped around the facial nerve. It was also good news that my facial nerve was NOT damaged or cut during the surgery. My facial nerve was intact, as was my bilateral hearing. I now have tinnitus on both sides, but we knew from the start that it would occur. The vestibular nerve was traumatized from the surgery, as expected, but I could make improvements in that area through vestibular therapy. These were particularly good results; however, recovery was still going to be quite a long road.

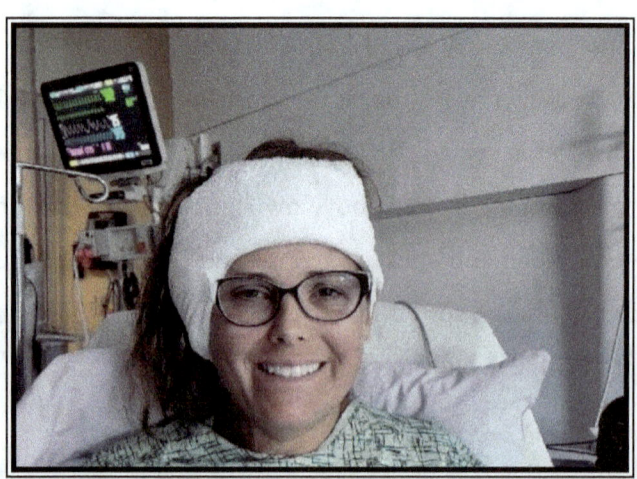

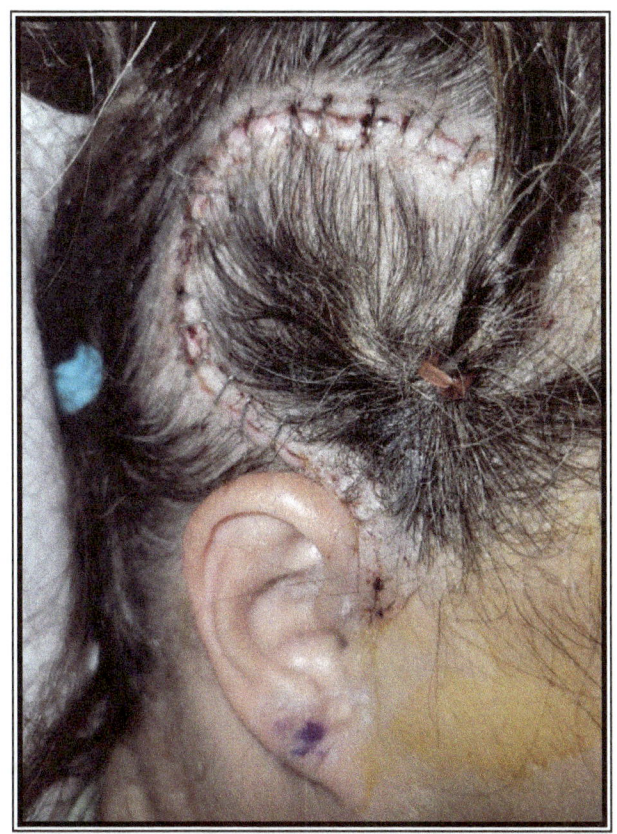

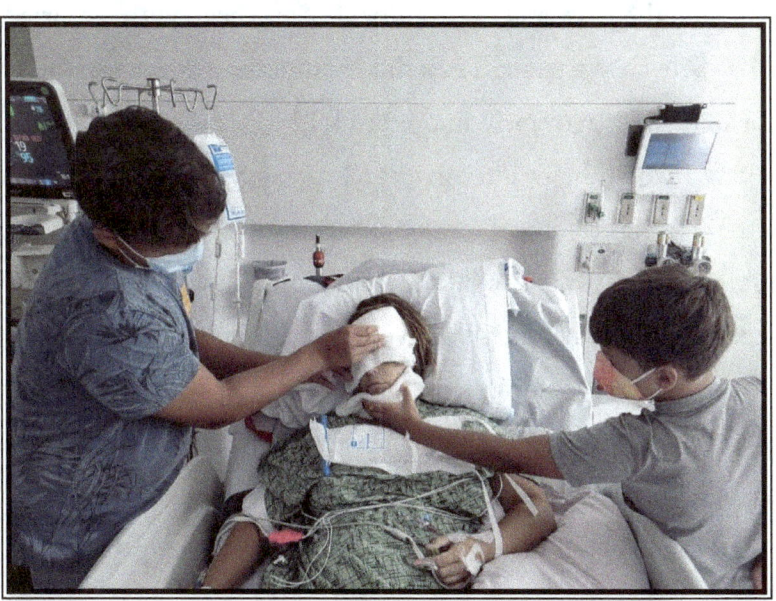

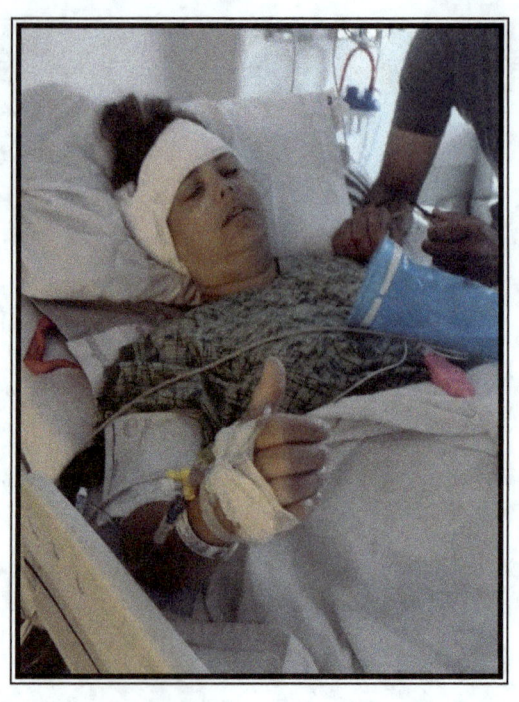

If you have been diagnosed with an acoustic neuroma and are looking for medical facilities to have a tumor removed, I would highly recommend the University of California-San Diego with Dr. Friedman and Dr. Schwartz's team. They did a fantastic job getting the entire tumor out. I was extremely impressed with their accurate estimates of how long I would be in intensive care, moving out of it and then back into the hospital/campus housing. There was also a wonderful nurse, Teresa, who we worked with and who would later send a message to the hospital recommending her to receive an outstanding nurse award. She was from Poland originally and had such a beautiful accent. She was the kindest and most considerate woman, and I teared up even thinking of her and her kindness. She would come into my room at all hours of the day and night, help make me more comfortable, and ask about my children and my life. She had a wonderful smile and seemed to enjoy hearing my ideas and thoughts of my sons. She explained that she also had a son, who was now a young adult, but she remembered what it was like raising him and being so close. I looked forward to seeing her and was excited when it was her shift, and she would come in and check on me.

The worst part of the brain surgery experience was my first time trying to stand up after the surgery. When I opened my eyes in the recovery room, the wall before me would sway as if I were on a rocking boat. A long horizontal shelf on the wall would move up and down like we were on rocky waves on a ship in the ocean. I would close my eyes again and then try to feel more centered and to be less nauseous. The first time the physical therapist tried to have me move from the bed to the chair, I started projectile vomiting and had blood shooting out of both nostrils at the same time. I could not believe how far all these liquids were shooting out of me like geysers. I had trouble breathing because it felt like I was vomiting out of my mouth and nose at the same time. When this happened, my husband, mother, and father were in the room. The look on my mother's face was full of shock and fear. We ended up laughing about it later. I had never experienced something like that before in my life. I told her I felt like a character in *The Exorcist*. We were able to laugh about this after the fact. My mother mentioned this a few times after the surgery, asking if I remembered when I was vomiting, and blood was shooting out of my nose at the same time. Writing about this makes me smile, even though it was so horrifying.

Over the next two days, I went on to standing and getting out of bed, sitting in the chair, walking short distances with the gait belt, and then walking up and down the stairwells in the hospital with assistance. I was quite unsteady walking, but I had the support of loved ones all around me.

The second worst part of the surgery was the nightmares that I had once I was out of the hospital and back in the hospital/campus housing.

I have been a mental health therapist for over twenty years and have worked with many trauma survivors, particularly of sexual and physical abuse. The nightmares felt so real, and it was all kinds of abuse that was being perpetrated on *me*. Some of the images reminded me of what clients had reported in retelling their stories of sexual abuse. It was awful. I could not see the faces of these perpetrators, but I became very fearful of going to sleep at night. Finally, after about a week, the nightmares stopped. I did research trying to find out if others who have had acoustic neuroma surgery had these types of nightmares, and they reported that many had. Most people think that this is due to the numerous medications and anesthesia used during the surgery.

Over the years, I learned how not to let the emotional and traumatic stories filter into my personal life and to compartmentalize the traumatic material from seeping into my mind. The period of nightmares made me wonder how all these past stories were creeping into my psyche and tormenting me while I was trying to recover from brain surgery.

*A sand tray miniature in my office reminds
me of the figures in my nightmares.*

The nightmares started when I left the hospital and was not so heavily medicated. We were back in the campus/hospital apartment. I would have them at night, not during the day when I was napping. I felt like I knew the stories and the perpetrators involved in these nightmares where someone was being sexually victimized and how. And that someone was me. I knew these stories, the graphic details, and what would happen. I could not see faces, and the figures were more like black blobs than human figures, but I was very aware of what was going to happen because I had heard and felt all of this before running my therapy sessions. Could I keep this all contained without these experiences seeping into my consciousness? I had felt like in my first few years as a mental health therapist, and I had learned to master keeping work at the office and not letting traumatic stories permeate into my everyday life and relationships. What shifted during the brain surgery?

The brain surgery involved the nerve running from my ear to my brain, and the inner brain structures were not disturbed during this surgery. But I find the nightmares very peculiar. The nightmares were like stories that I had heard before and felt before in my therapy sessions with trauma victims; such an odd phenomenon. Had I accidentally opened some floodgate into traumatic memories that I had experienced with clients but had tried to contain so cleanly for many years? I am not sure. But luckily, these horrible nightmares ceased about a week after surgery. I will die a happy woman if I never have one of these nightmares again.

I was sad and frustrated that I was trying to recover from brain surgery and facing so many memories of vicarious sexual abuse as well. It was a double whammy. I am glad that chapter in my life is over. I am not sure how much more I could have endured. But I guess we never know how much we can endure until we are put to the test.

The nightmares were of me being assaulted and objects being forced into my body. Could this have been about my brain surgery experience? I am not sure, but it is interesting that other brain surgery patients have reported horrific nightmares as well.

I felt solace in reading. It was particularly important to me to have novels to read at night with a book light. The rest of my family, my two sons, and husband, slept for the night. I would stay up reading to postpone having these nightmares the entire first week of recovery in California. After the nightmares stopped, I was able to sleep better.

Reading has always been important to me. Nothing is more relaxing and fulfilling than reading a good book and escaping to the story or places while staying in your own home. I was pleasantly surprised to see that I could still read and enjoy many books.

We went to Target in La Jolla to get me a book light to read at night when the others were sleeping. This was my first *big store* experience after the surgery. We were looking at the shelves and all the items were so bright and busy that I had to look away. It was completely overwhelming to me. I started sweating and my head started hurting even more. I even felt a little nauseous. We asked a sales clerk where the book lights would be in the store. He looked it up on his Target gadget and told us the correct aisle. I thanked him and almost ran off to get to that part of the store, trying to get out of this overstimulating circus as soon as possible. Once in the right section, we still could not find the book light. I felt like I was going to have a panic attack. The kids were getting distracted and looking at other items of interest. I said, "We NEED to find the book light and exit as soon as possible." I could not take being in that store a minute longer. Luckily, the book light was found, and we left the box store quickly. This was going to be something I would have to get used to. The normal everyday routine of going to a big store with fluorescent lighting and overstimulation.

I have come full circle with reading in my life. As a child, I had difficulty with reading, and my aunt Debbie (who was in school to be a teacher) would take me with her and work on reading and flashcards she was making in her courses. I remember going to the laundromat, and while she washed her clothes, we would practice reading and work with her reading flashcards. What a wonderful aunt and a lovely memory. I ended up progressing from the remedial reading class to the advanced reading group in my elementary school. My Aunt Debbie passed away at age forty-nine from liver cancer and breast cancer; what a shame. She was a wonderful human being. I wish she were here to read my first book.

I feel at peace while reading. It has not been affected by my surgery the way my hearing was. If I do not feel well enough to go out and about, I enjoy staying home and reading. Now, I am writing my first book as a way to work more from home and switch gears in my professional life. I would have never known how important those visits to the laundromat for working on reading would be in my adult life. Thank you, Aunt Debbie.

Who are the influential people that come to mind in your life? Maybe a family member, teacher, neighbor, coach, family friend, boss, or coworker? Take a moment to think about how this person contributed to the person you are today.

CHAPTER 14

Steps Back into the Real World

It was explained to me that I was ready to leave the intensive care part of the hospital. My choice was to either go to the next step down in the hospital or to go back to the campus/hospital apartments because I had so many people there to help me. It felt good knowing that my loved ones were there to help and that I could move to the apartment with my husband and boys and leave the hospital. While on the recovery floor and after discharge, I learned to walk with a gait belt. We were told to be as active as possible but not to overdo it. They suggested multiple short walks per day and then resting in between. The physical therapist assessed what the proper amount would be. I needed to push myself physically, but if I pushed too hard, I would not progress either. I had to find the right balance. I was learning that this was the recurring theme in my life for the past twenty years.

The heavy-duty gait belt was around my waist, with my husband holding on to it and helping guide me so he could hold me up if I started to fall. The belt seemed like such a small, flimsy apparatus to keep me from falling. The person working with me had to be strong to keep me up and moving. I had to trust that they would not let me fall. The gait belt was just a tool, but the real guidance came from the supportive people around me. Learning to walk again took the correct balance of push and pull between the two partners. This screams metaphorically about marriage partners of twenty-three years.

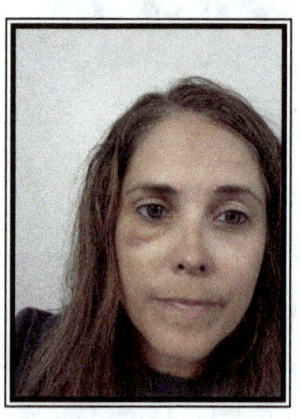

This makes me think about people who may not have family members to come along and help them if they need this intensive surgery. From my different acoustic neuroma groups, I have learned from others that often, a good friend will accompany them, or if that is not an option, a nurse or nursing assistant could be hired to help with the recovery/rehabilitation process after surgery. You cannot be independent right out of the gate, so having that supportive person or people is so important. This statement makes me think of the various young children I have worked with in my counseling/play therapy practice over the years. They cannot be independent and there is so much to learn and support needed to be given by their support person, whether this is a parent, grandparent, foster parent, caring neighbor, teacher, etc.

One caring adult is all it takes to help a child succeed.

My husband and boys would take me for walks, and we were able to build up to four short walks a day. We took two walks in the morning and two in the afternoon. I usually slept between these walks. One morning, my foot hit a cement retaining wall near the sidewalk, and I fell. This was a bit of a surprise to me, but I just got back up. It was harder to catch myself if I started to get off balance due to my vestibular nerve being traumatized in the surgery. I often grabbed my husband or sons on these walks if I felt off balance. In the past, we hiked in the Black Hills, where my family lives, downhill skied, and did an occasional fun run with friends. I have always felt that I was physically strong. But these walks were exceedingly difficult post-surgery. So many things were off-kilter in my hearing and balance system. I could not tell which way the sound was coming from. If I tried to turn my head to look for an oncoming car or other distraction, I would wobble and lose my balance. Doing two things at once was very difficult.

There was a parking ramp that we walked through on our way to a part of the college campus. The noises, dark and light, and moving cars were very unnerving. I would feel completely overstimulated sensory-wise and would want to hold on to someone steady because I could not trust my balance or keep myself safe from sights and sounds that were coming out of nowhere. Stepping up onto a curb took more concentration than walking straight, and if I had to step up on a curb and look sideways for a car approaching, this was more than I could do. When we walked by other pedestrians, I could not turn my head or say hello because I would lose concentration and balance. If I tried to look up at the sky, I would also lose my balance unless I was holding on to someone. I felt like I was trying to walk while intoxicated, and it looked as though I was intoxicated as well! I am glad this campus was well known for brain surgery and for helping people learn to balance and walk again.

We were walking one evening as it was getting dark. The kids were playing around on some younger kids' playground equipment by the hospital. As it got darker, I was no longer in control and could fall at any minute. I kept my gaze down, watching my feet and then watching my boys ahead of me in single file down these paths, eager to make it home to the apartment. *One step at a time and stay close to the people helping you.*

My walks progressed throughout the days that we were in the Family Apartments. First, I would have to go and sleep after returning from a short walk. As the days passed and I became stronger and more acclimated vestibularly, I would still have energy when I returned from a walk and could stay awake and interact with my boys and husband. My husband is quite an athlete and competitive. One day, we took a longer walk, discovered more about the campus, and bought a few items at a small store there. This was a big step in knowing that I was improving each day and making gains in small ways.

Another small victory was when I used a public restroom in the small campus grocery store and was able to lift up my leg high to flush the toilet with my foot instead of touching the public toilet handle with my hand. Now, that was an advanced physical therapy move!

CHAPTER 15

Vestibular Issues

Vestibular issues cause symptoms of vertigo, dizziness, balance problems, intolerance to head motion, unsteady gait, and nausea. Vestibular therapy encourages head and eye movements to get back in sync.

I started vestibular therapy as soon as I was able to step out of my hospital bed. I was learning in the hallways, holding onto the IV pole. Once I *mastered* this, I would walk up and down the stairwells of the hospital with my physical therapist and my husband. In a brief time, I made substantial progress and felt that walking would become manageable again. My husband and boys would take me on four short walks around the campus daily. I would be tired out from all the sensory issues very quickly. At this point, I had been in intensive care in the hospital, the campus housing apartment, and now I was starting to think about the long plane ride home.

Vestibular Physical Therapy Following Surgery: Patient Guide to Recovery and Home Exercise Program

On August 24, 2022, we had five postoperative appointments at the University of California - San Diego eight days after my surgery. I have partial hearing loss in my right ear now (tumor side), but they reported that it could bounce back in the next two months. The doctors reported that a hearing aid would be an option. My sensory overload could balance out over the next two months. I was grateful for the tumor to be out! Now, for the long road to recovery and rehabilitation.

The rooftop deck of the La Jolla Family
Housing on our last night in California.

We were all very excited to get back home.

CHAPTER 16

Heading Home

We flew home from San Diego nine days after the surgery on August 25, 2022. Walking through the airport felt like a weird video game to me. Escalators and running walkways were difficult for me. I chose not to have a wheelchair provided by the airport because walking was more comfortable than riding with bumps, sharp turns, and stops. It would be easier if I could control my movement at this point. The beeping of the golf carts, taking people to and fro, was too much for my head. Our flight was delayed numerous times, and my luggage was lost. I almost felt delirious when they said my luggage was lost. "I remember saying I don't even care about my luggage. Everything in there can be replaced. I want to go home." I was so grateful to be home!

Flying home from California after the brain surgery.

I was amazed by the kindness of friends and family upon my return home.

I was so excited to see my eldest son when we returned home. I hugged him with all my might. It had been three weeks since I had seen him. My firstborn, I felt complete being back near him again. My friends and family had decorated my front porch with mums, balloons, and other flowers. It looked so welcoming, and I could not wait to get back inside my own home.

I had never been away from my son Henry for that long of a time. Hugging him was the best thing about being home. This boy had made me a mother, and I did not feel complete with him being absent from my life for so long. I was back with my oldest son. I felt like I could breathe again.

My friends had organized a meal train to help feed my family for the next couple of months. This was such a gift because, with three boys, someone is always hungry in our home. My family benefited from all the meals and desserts brought to our door, and we felt very loved.

I continued vestibular physical therapy with our local provider soon after I returned home to Rapid City. My physical therapy sessions comprised different balancing activities: walking activities, riding a stationary bike, walking on a line, balancing with my feet in various positions, walking outside on the grass and hillside, stepping up onto curbs outdoors, and so on. There was also a machine where I stood on a platform that would tilt at odd angles, and I tried to keep my balance on the moving box. There was a screen where my score would tally regarding how I had done in certain areas. I improved with this box exercise with my eyes open, but it was exceedingly difficult with my eyes closed. If my eyes were closed, it would be extremely hard for me to keep my balance. After these sessions, I would immediately go home and go to sleep because my brain was so tired. My kids got used to seeing me sleep. I would excuse myself, go upstairs to my bedroom, and sleep many hours daily. My parents would take me to physical therapy sessions because I was not yet driving, and my husband needed to be at work. We were a family of five without sick leave because we owned two small businesses.

In my research, I found claims that acupuncture could help the body heal and become more balanced. My acupuncturist explained that the blood flow was a bit off on the left side of my body, especially my arm, which had been hurting so much directly after the surgery. She inserted needles into my skin, focusing a lot on the blood flow on the left side to help get my pulse back to normal. I also continued to have skin lesions, and they were strangely more on the left side of my body. The brain surgery was on the right side. I found this interesting and wondered about the connection.

As part of my recovery, I needed to keep my head elevated higher than my heart while sleeping for two weeks. It was much easier sleeping in a recliner once I returned home. My three boys moved that recliner I had in their bedroom to rock them to sleep when they were babies. I was now using this recliner in my bedroom to sleep for my recovery. In a way, we had changed roles in the family. I was sleeping several hours during the day. They tried to be quiet, not to wake me if I was asleep. I had done these same things with the three of them, putting them down for naptime each day and rocking them in the big brown rocker recliner. I will always smile about three strong boys moving the recliner into my room. I have often had fond memories of rocking them to sleep at night or sleeping there to be near them when they were ill. These big, burly boys were carrying this recliner to my bedroom for me.

On one of the first nights I was home, I woke up and the bedroom curtain looked very odd. I got up in my pajamas, felt the material, and laughed at myself because I knew that curtain was fine; it was just how my brain was seeing/perceiving it. It looked as if the curtain was moving like a waterfall. I knew it was not and felt like I was on some street drugs or something. I laughed and went back to bed. I am sure my husband would have wondered what was going on if he had woken up and I was standing in our bedroom holding the curtain in awe with my eyes big and my mouth agape.

Another vestibular issue was when I woke up in the morning, I would think I was hearing my alarm clock. When I lifted my head so both ears could hear, the beeping was not my alarm clock, but it was pulsating tinnitus that sounded like an alarm clock. This was very frustrating because it would wake me up incredibly early, before I needed to get up, around 4:00 A.M. When my alarm clock went off, my husband would have to nudge me because I could no longer hear my alarm clock with my right ear. I usually sleep on my left side (which became a habit during my pregnancies), so my good ear was down. At first, my husband seemed a little frustrated, but then he realized I could no longer hear my alarm clock. Tinnitus, at times, changed to a loud sound, as if someone was scraping metal together, and it was a blood-curdling sound. When my head became this loud, I would again check out and sleep.

Regarding vision, when I first woke up, the exposed wooden beams on our bedroom ceiling would turn in a circular pattern. I would take a deep breath, close my eyes again, and hope I would be more balanced and the wood beams would no longer be turning when I opened my eyes again. I would try to focus intently on one wood beam until it would stay stationary. My new normal consisted of different perceptual distortions, like shadows in my room. What may have been frightening turned into a more humorous situation I was curious about. Focusing on the wood beams until they were no longer turning each morning was a sort of litmus test for getting out of bed. This would happen daily after surgery, and the spinning has decreased in the past year.

The curtains and wood beams in my bedroom at home, where I spent many hours sleeping for my recovery.

Tinnitus

I started categorizing tinnitus into three different gradients to describe what I was experiencing.

- *Low-Grade Tinnitus*

Automatically, it is ignored by the brain in most situations.

It sounds like static from an old-fashioned television or a white noise machine.

- *Medium-Grade Tinnitus*

The tinnitus is louder, and you are more aware of it happening in your brain.

My head starts to feel a little tired and off balance at this stage, usually mid-day.

- *High-Grade Tinnitus*

This is when the sound becomes so loud that it is physically hard to listen to people and tune in to what others are saying. My brain felt exhausted, and my best choice was to close my eyes and sleep.

Barometric pressure changes or storms affect tinnitus levels (for me).

Later in my journey, I discovered that a hearing aid could help with my tinnitus.

Back to Work

At about six weeks post-surgery, I went back to work. I had been doing a few telehealth counseling sessions from home on the computer and knew my brain was functioning properly again to talk and counsel people. It felt great being able to shower on my own, wash my hair, and get ready for the day. I liked being out in the community meeting with many of my clients who knew I was on leave for brain surgery and had been praying and thinking of me as well. I was happy to be interacting with people again. I love my career and was happy to be back at the office and out of my t-shirts and sweatpants. My career gives me a sense of purpose. I would come to see that I would need to find various ways to find purpose in the next chapter.

CHAPTER 17

Change in Perspective

When I was in graduate school, we spent a great deal of time discussing how human beings start to look at the big picture when they experience hardship. Am I focusing on the right things in my life? How could my life be more genuine? How can I be more present? What is holding me back from living that life? How do I get around these obstacles? What patterns do I have that do not suit me well? We had several short vacations planned for the summer after my brain surgery. My parents and sister sat me down and talked to me about canceling a vacation to Colorado because I had been ill most of the week and sleeping many hours when I would return home from work. My sister commented on how it seemed like I was running in a hamster wheel and not getting to where I wanted to be. She explained that I work a lot of hours, and then I feel so exhausted that I must sleep for many hours. Although I was initially surprised to hear this, after thinking it over, I realized my sister had a point. I had a pattern of overdoing things, projects, parties, baking, and decorating with Christmas lights. I try to do things well- go big or go home. I love to take my kids on vacation. I like to have fun and excitement. I have had a pattern of working too many hours and having trouble saying no.

This has been a pattern in my life. I felt very good about being a hard worker and working until a job was complete, putting in more hours and effort, whatever it took to succeed at my goal. This was now a part of the problem instead of the solution. I had to evaluate this and how I was going to go about changing it.

But over time, I have made real changes. I am now getting to a point where I am feeling so content staying in my beautiful home for the day, walking my dog, reading in a quiet room, and writing this book. My new brain needs me not to go so fast and to slow down.

I realized I needed to shift my thinking and downsize my plans and schedule. I was a year out from surgery and thought I would be able to handle all my old responsibilities like before, but I was exhausted and slept a large amount of the time when I was home. This schedule was not working. I had received the wake-up call. I no longer plan and host big parties. It is too much work and stimulation. I prefer having a night at home with my family watching a movie or an outing to a coffee shop with a friend. I have greatly decreased going shopping at large box stores because I do not feel regulated and balanced afterward. I will do this once in a while, but I really have to want to embark on the shopping outing.

My husband's problem-solving approach is like mine: work hard and continue until the job is done. He had not said anything to me about this pattern because he may have this pattern, too. I was raised learning that having an excellent work ethic and being a hard worker were one of the best traits possible. But I needed to take an intermission and re-evaluate what was working for me with this new brain and what was no longer working for me. But coming to this realization was the easy part. After identifying this, the hard part was changing the lifelong pattern.

Speaking of patterns, my husband has a pattern of being strong and not letting anyone think you may be suffering or need support. This might be because he is one of five boys, all great athletes. I was amazed how, when we learned about the tumor, he would tell people I was fine, he was fine, everything was fine. I did not want to play the victim, but everything was far from fine. Since the surgery, my husband can talk more about things that are not fine. Sometimes, people are hurt, and it is okay to talk about this. He has seen the love and generosity of many friends and family who have come to help in every possible way. He saw how their love and support kept me going and helped raise my spirits at some of my lowest points. This has also changed my children and the way they view life. I feel closer to my husband when he can acknowledge what is happening in real life and not put up the stoic wall. Some great changes took place throughout this family and individual medical crisis. Traumatic events affect people in all kinds of ways. This certainly is not something I would wish upon my family, but it happened, and we handled it the best way we knew—by being together.

"We were together. I forget the rest."

-Walt Whitman

If I could do it over again, I am not sure the boys would have seen me so soon when I got out of surgery. One of my boys had flashbacks of my post-surgery face every night when he was trying to fall asleep. He stated how horrible I looked, corpse-like, and it was very frightening to see his mother this way. I was not conscious at this point, so I do not remember them seeing me. But when I hear my son talk about this, I would do it differently or advise other acoustic neuroma patients to do that differently so that the image is not etched in their child's mind. Another thought, though, is the opposite: Kids can grow stronger in dealing with difficult things and seeing how they improve. This is the hard part of being a parent. You want to protect your kids from the hard things in life, but they also need to learn that life can be hard and how to use healthy coping strategies to deal with the hard parts of this world.

Seeking Help

I also felt comfortable bringing my boys to therapy to talk with a licensed child/adolescent therapist about their thoughts and feelings regarding our traumatic situation. I am a mental health counselor, and I have a specialty in working with children and families. It was time for me to be on the other side of the office wall and bring my child/children to therapy to have someone they could talk to about this confusing situation, who was not their parent. I am grateful for helping professionals who were able to be available for my children and our family to help us through this ordeal.

I have been in counseling as well to process the stress and life changes and try to change my perspective. I continued in individual therapy for myself to process and learn to cope with all of the changes in my "new normal," I could learn to ADAPT and focus on my strengths.

Sand tray (therapy technique)

Sand tray therapy is very powerful and one of my favorite modalities in therapy. I created this sand tray in my office during an open hour in my work day. The one on the previous page depicts the journey of the acoustic neuroma through symbols (sand tray miniatures). The picture on the right expresses the feelings associated with the situation with the feeling stones.

My boys have learned to be very empathetic and caring towards others and the challenging times that others are going through. Teachers have told me how they are very understanding to other students at school, notice who may be hurting, and try to help. My boys are more comfortable talking about feelings and what may not be working so well.

My sons pick up heavy items for me because even a year out, the right side of my brain gets a high-pitched sound if I lift something too heavy.

Also, if I rub my head, I get a high-pitched sound on the right side of my head. It is like a crazy, fun house in my skull, and I tell my family about the odd sounds! If it is dark out, I hold onto one of their arms because it is hard for me to balance walking in the dark. It is getting better, and I hope my recovery continues into my second year.

Easy applicable activities to help change your perspective after a life-changing event:

1. Circle of control activities

   List what you are in control of in one circle and what you have no control over in the other circle

2. Bridge activity

   Label on the boards of the bridge steps you need to take to get to your desired goal

3. Identifying your circles of support

   We all have people who are important to us and very supportive, and some who are not. Write the supportive names of people in the inner circle and acquaintances or people who are not as supportive in the outer circle.

These handouts are available to print at my website: www.LP-publishing.com

Example:

What I Can Control

- My effort
- Vestibular therapy
- Walking each day
- Breath work or meditation
- Reducing my "to do" list
- Trying to see the good

What I Cannot Control

- How I feel physically each day
- That I have an acoustic neuroma
- Other people
- The weather (barometric changes)

Fill in for your situation

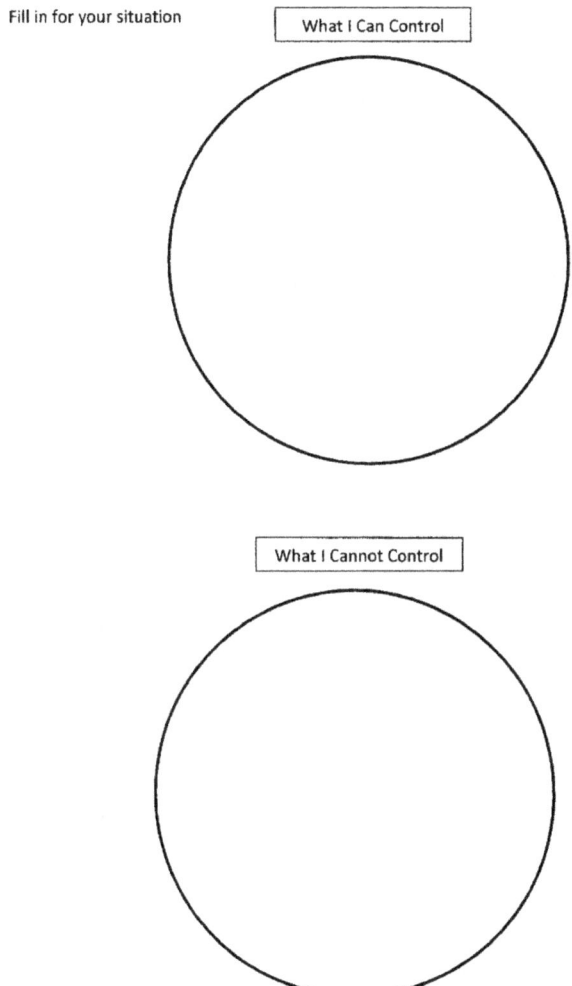

What I Can Control

What I Cannot Control

Write in the steps it will take to get from where you are currently to where you want to be.

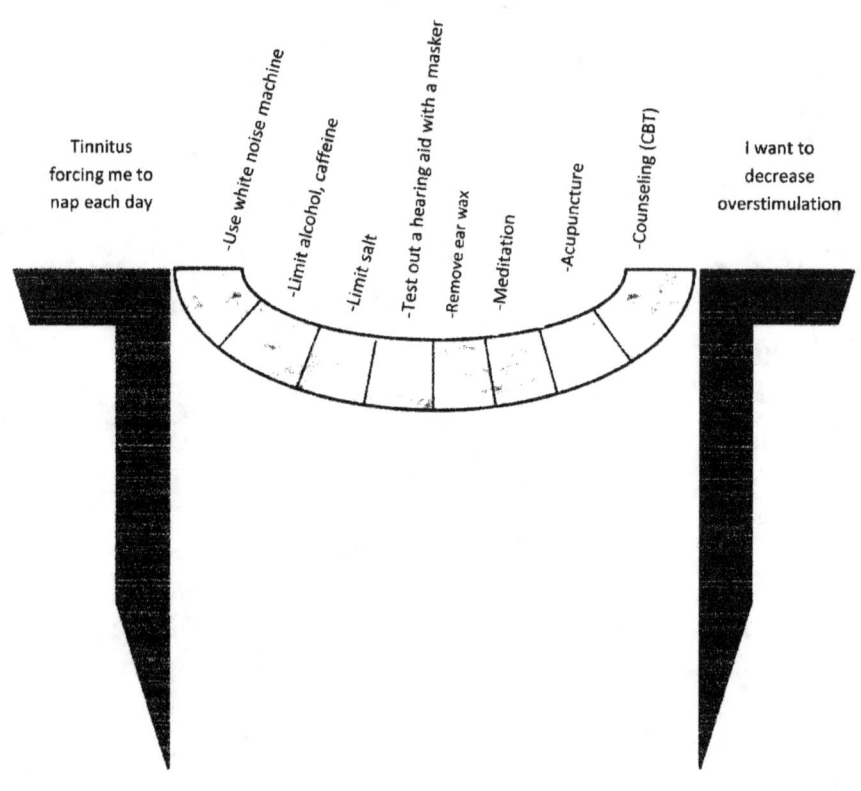

Tinnitus forcing me to nap each day

- Use white noise machine
- Limit alcohol, caffeine
- Limit salt
- Test out a hearing aid with a masker
- Remove ear wax
- Meditation
- Acupuncture
- Counseling (CBT)

I want to decrease overstimulation

Write in the steps it will take to get from where you are currently to where you want to be.

Where I am
currently

Where I want
to be

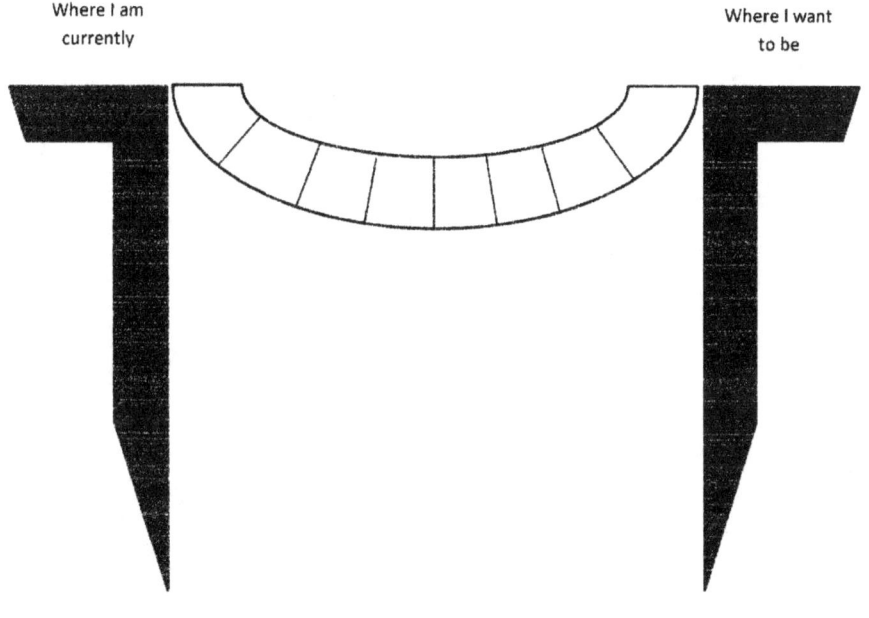

Your Support System

- Who is in your inner circle, write names of closest friends and family members
- Who is in your outer circle, write names of other supportive people in your life

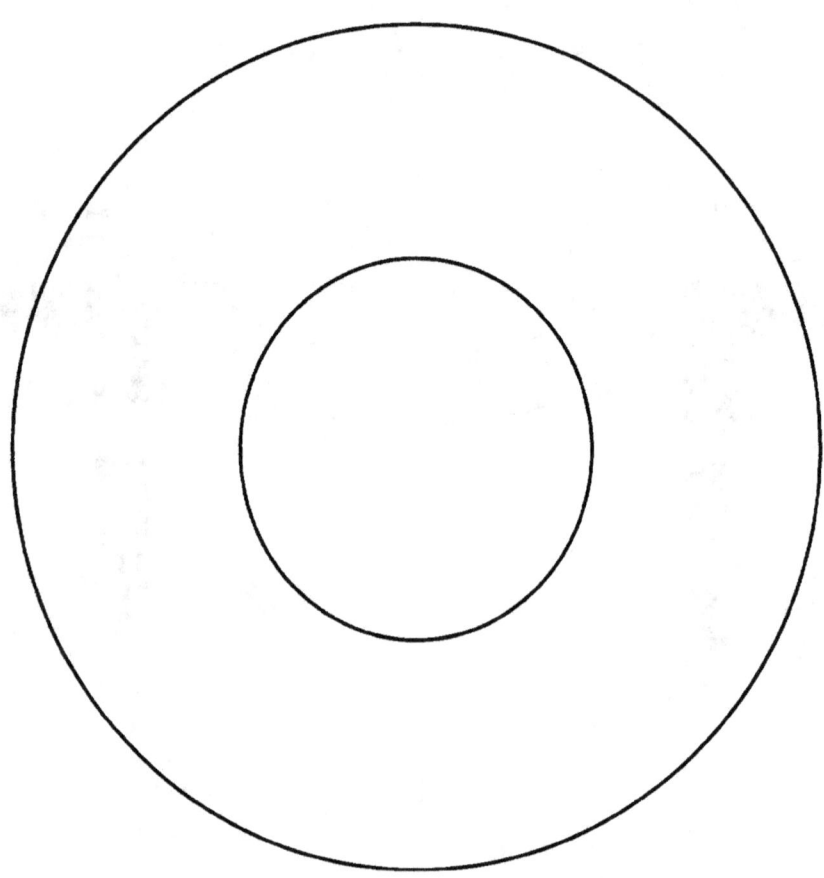

PART 3

CHAPTER 18

A Year Out from Surgery

It had been a year since my craniotomy to remove my acoustic neuroma. It had been a progression for the past year, with one step forward and then two steps back. I was feeling very frustrated during the winter months. We have a lot of snow and barometric pressure changes in the Black Hills of South Dakota. It felt like I was calling in sick to work at least a day or two a week. It is essential to be reliable and consistent as a mental health therapist, and this was not happening due to my brain surgery recovery. On the days when the weather was not changing, I would get sick or a cold from one of the clients coming in to see me at my business. I work with many children, and it is exceedingly difficult to keep them healthy in the winter. The common cold annoyed the normal person, but it would put me in bed for the day due to vestibular issues and inability to balance or concentrate. Around March 2022, I told my husband, "I am at my limit."

I told him that I could not do this anymore. I was feeling sick and dizzy constantly and could not figure out how to make this new normal work. I felt depressed when I could not be out doing what I wanted to do and spending so much time sleeping. He told me, "Well, you have no choice but to keep going."

I eventually made it through the winter. We planned a trip to Jamaica for the boys' spring break from school at the end of March. I did not have headaches or noticeable tinnitus in Jamaica. I have always loved the ocean, but being near it with all its waves crashing was wonderful. I did not hear my tinnitus at all, only waves and seagulls. The weather was warm; we spent a lot of time in the sun and ocean, and I napped when needed. What a rejuvenating trip. But who would not feel better in Jamaica? At this point, I felt like I could make it to summer, and my spirits were lifting.

Jamaica April 2023

I was looking forward to summer because I love to be outside and in the sun. My boys would be home from school and relaxing, and hopefully, we would have a lot of time to enjoy the outdoors and weather. Our part of the country is known for being in droughts often. I was ready and waiting for the steady, sunny weather. However, we had one of the rainiest summers ever in the Black Hills of South Dakota. I had to nap often and again felt like my life was "on hold" until the weather would be steadier. On days when the weather was constant, with no storms, and I still felt exhausted, I told my sister, "I have no idea at this point. Maybe the stars were aligned in a certain way today." I would laugh to keep myself from crying. I could not find a pattern of why my head was heavy and where the excruciating tinnitus was coming from some days.

I had scheduled the one-year follow-up head MRI many months ahead of time, wanting to find out as soon as possible if the tumor was growing back or not. My husband accompanied me to the appointment, and I was ready to find more answers. This time, I did not ask for any medications for anxiety. I figured I would make it through this MRI fine. I was starting to feel like I could handle anything at this point. We would find out the outcome of the MRI that week. At the local imaging clinic, a prisoner was waiting for imaging, and he had shackles and chains with a police officer on each side. I chuckled in my head, thinking that things could be worse: I could be a prisoner and have a rare tumor that I was hoping was not growing back!

People often say that things could always be worse when someone is going through a tough time. I heard this often about my tumor because it was not cancerous, and we were lucky we caught it when it was small. Or that getting Covid was for the best because it helped us find the tumor when my ear would not stop ringing. There is another side, too, though. What if Covid accelerated the symptomology? Many people live with acoustic neuromas for years; they stay small and do not have many symptoms. These people would decide the route, watch and wait, because their quality of life is not affected much.

I was hoping that after I had the tumor out and spent a year recovering, most of my symptoms would have been gone. They have drastically improved but are still present to a lesser degree.

The doctors were hopeful that most of my symptoms would disappear. We always knew that my tinnitus would not improve either way. Each patient is different, and people have different results from the surgery and year of recovery. Most literature states that improvements occur in the first two years, so I have another year to see if there are more gains. The doctors had explained this to me, but everyone is different in their surgery and recovery. Patients must wait and see how many improvements they have after the surgery. There are no guarantees. But it is a relief to me to know that the tumor is out.

Another worry that I had been having was that I might have the diagnosis of Neurofibromatosis Type 2. In an earlier chapter, I explained that this neurofibromatosis tumor can be passed down genetically. However, 50 percent of the people who have NF2 do not have parents who have NF2 but rather a spontaneous genetic mutation. All the medical teams had asked if I had a history of NF2 in my family during our consultations, but I have no relatives with this disorder, so we just moved on. The only reason I was worried about NF2 is that there can be skin lesions that accompany an acoustic neuroma. With NF2, tumors grow on both sides of the body. I only had a tumor on the right side.

The skin lesions have not gone away after a year and a half of treatment. The diagnosis of my skin lesions is lichen planus. Lichen planus is an inflammatory skin condition of the skin and mucous membranes. The immune system mistakenly attacks the cells of your own body. The skin disorder, again, is rare. People develop splotches that turn to dark spots (almost maroon for me) along their torso, armpits, and inside my mouth. There is no known cause for lichen planus and no known cure. Different dermatological creams and medications can help, but no well-known treatment works for everyone. Lichen planus can become skin cancer if not managed and monitored by a dermatologist. So, I have a stubborn case of lichen planus.

In the MRI machine this time around, I did shed tears. I was thinking about my sons and that I would take any illness, but please spare my sons from having to go through this. I was starting to think that I might have NF2 because the skin lesions were not going away, and I had them in my mouth as well. When medical providers tell me that I do not have a condition because it is extremely rare, it has become a trigger phrase for me to flood with anxiety because the tumor was rare. Lichen planus has a higher probability of turning into skin cancer if the person has it in their mouth, and I did have it in my mouth.

I am a mental health therapist and work with clients to reduce anxiety. One of the techniques is to think about the probability of an adverse event happening to help decrease anxious thoughts. Well, in the last two years, I have been experiencing a lot of *rare* conditions. The word "rare" was triggering me more than calming my mind.

Why would I want to know if I did have NF2 if there was no treatment and nothing that I could do about it? If a treatment came about to help people with this condition, then I would want to know so my children would have a leg up on combating this disorder. But as of right now, there is no cure for this disorder. I have already had the acoustic neuroma tumor removed, I was having the skin issues treated and monitored, even if it was not going away. If I started to develop tumors on both sides of my brain or spinal cord, then I would know I did have NF2.

Would you want to know if you had an untreatable condition and if there was nothing you could do about it? What a question to think about and ponder. Or would you rather go out and try to live your life to the best of your ability? That week, our local imaging center informed me that the MRI results showed no re-growth of the tumor and no traces of any other tumors. This was fabulous news regarding the acoustic neuroma being dormant and the very unlikely potential of having NF2—finally, some relief.

A weight is lifted

When I awoke the next morning, I had a sense of calm I had not felt in ages. I had never mentioned this to anyone because it was such a fleeting and quick feeling. I had this feeling like I was falling (anxiety) when I woke up most mornings. The panic would take over for a split second, and then I would think, *What do I need to do today to get back on track and be able to have a day without struggles?* I would get up and do my walking outside with my dog, do my vestibular exercises, get my boys out the door, do my morning meditation, and then I would get to my office.

This first morning after the clear MRI results, I felt so grateful that this saga was finally over and I could continue with my life as I knew it pre-tumor. I felt for the first time that everything would be alright. A feeling of peace and contentment that is hard to describe. Not just the verbiage but believing this in my heart. If only this would have been the final word about the one-year follow-up MRI.

The Calm After the Storm

I took a deep breath and told myself, finally believing *I am going to be okay.* This is done and over. Onward, to raise my sons and see what kind of adventures they will have in the world. My husband and I will be able to retire and travel to far-off lands someday in the future together.

CHAPTER 19

News from California

received a call from California from the physician's assistant, Tamara, whom I really liked when we were at UC San Diego. She explained that Dr. Schwartz had reviewed my one-year follow-up MRI results and that he noted a *linear enhancement*. She explained that this meant that the MRI noticed a denser area of cells in my brain. This enhancement could be from postoperative reactivity, a tumor, infection, or some other abnormality. She did not want me to worry too much about it, but they wanted me to get my next MRI in one year instead of five years to monitor it more closely.

This phone call was a blow because I had already received word from the imaging center in our city that my MRI looked clear the previous week. I thought that was the final word, but now I realized that Rapid City thought the MRI looked fine but that UC San Diego (the specialists) saw an abnormality in the image. I did not get emotional about this. I felt numb, like whatever was going to happen was going to happen. At this point, I was thinking I may not choose to have brain surgery again if it was another tumor.

I also talked with Tamara about how I had been having a tough year, expecting to be further along in my recovery one year out. I explained to her that I was still taking a one to two-hour nap most days after work to function the rest of the evening. I told her I was walking each morning as directed and felt good in the mornings, but the ringing in my ear and balance really got out of order in the afternoon/ evening after I had been up for several hours. She suggested that I start my vestibular therapy again, and maybe that will help improve the situation. She agreed that cutting back and having less stress and busyness would also be beneficial. She also wanted me to schedule another MRI in one year to monitor the linear enhancement.

I started taking two days off at this time to see if the ringing and balance troubles would decrease if I were working less and seeing fewer clients in my therapy office. It would be an experiment to see what was most taxing to my brain. The new obstacle at my counseling clinic seemed to be the *sensory overload* from listening and feeling so heavily (being attuned) to what my clients were saying. The nerve between my ear and my brain is where the tumor was located and extracted. My clinical counseling skills depend on the functioning of that area. Listening was my number one asset in my career. My career was listening, understanding, being attuned, and helping people find a path that works better for them or processing past difficulties/trauma.

I already told my kids that the MRI was clear, and we had all celebrated and felt some closure. I was unsure what to tell them at this point, whether I should correct the information or just wait to see what the next MRI would indicate. I started to feel that I just needed to try to live my life because I was not sure about the future again.

I will have another MRI in August of 2024 to see a clearer picture of the small mass of cells that was spotted in my brain on this year's MRI. Hopefully, it will not accumulate too much of anything, but it is hard to know what the future holds. I started thinking about how many people do not know what the next year has in store for them either. We all just try to live our lives meaningfully and have a life worth living.

The key to being prepared for the unknown isn't about predicting the future, but about developing an unwavering resilience and composure to confront whatever may arise.

-Marcus Aurelius

The day after talking to the University of California San Diego, I started my vestibular therapy exercises again in addition to the walking that I needed to do each morning. By the time I was ready to work, I was already pretty tired. I told myself that I could do this, though. I would work every other day instead of five days a week, and I could make this work. I can continue to work and try to get back to the best new normal possible. Maybe doing more vestibular therapy will help me get back to a good baseline and not need to nap each day when the ringing gets so loud. I asked Tamara if tinnitus typically gets louder throughout the day or if, with most people, tinnitus stays the same volume. She said everyone is different but thought tinnitus stayed the same volume, making it easier to block out.

She explained that I might benefit from a hearing aid in my right ear with a *masker* to help block out the changing volume of tinnitus in my head. I also asked her if the linear enhancement was on the left or right side of my brain. She stated that it was on the surgery side (right side), so I was excited that it was not NF2, which was my most significant concern, being passed on to my kids. I was excited to have a new lead that may improve my symptoms. I called the ENT clinic and was able to make an appointment a month out. Hopefully, I can get more answers and have a small device make a world of difference for me, my overstimulation, and my way of being.

My thinking had transformed during this time. I was no longer *waiting to hear how my life was going to turn out*, but I was going to try to just go live each day without so many demands. I would try to enjoy the little things. Even if another tumor grows back, it is not the end of the world. They are usually slow-growing tumors, and hell, I made it through one brain surgery. Or maybe I wouldn't even get brain surgery again. Perhaps I would do radiation for the next one if a next one exists. Older people can do radiation on these tumors, and if I let it grow for about ten years, I would be in the age category for radiation, which is less invasive. I jokingly told people that I was looking forward to getting older so I could choose radiation over brain surgery! I also read that the second time you have brain surgery, recovery happens much more quickly. Bingo! I will be fine! I started to get a sense of humor about this condition.

After talking to several doctors, they all agreed that I likely did not have NF2. Most people with NF2 are diagnosed at a much younger age, and I was too old! Oh my goodness, I'm too old to have the disease that could be passed down to my children. I'm getting older each day and that brings me closer to choosing radiation if there is another brain tumor. This was some pretty good news, and I now knew the ins and outs of getting through this medical problem.

Would you choose to find out if you had a life-threatening condition that had no cure? It is quite the question to think about. I would say this is the biggest boost to living mindfully and living each day like it is your last. A person would have a better quality of life with this mindset anyway.

CHAPTER 20

The Mind and Body Connection

$\mathcal{M}$any doctors told me that I was having trouble with inflammation in my body. This was contributing to my skin lesions (rash). I kept returning to the fact that something was attacking my body's soft tissue (mucous membranes). Could this be due to Covid, the Covid vaccine, one of the twenty medications I was on after surgery, or the prednisone I was on numerous times before we knew about the tumor? We know that steroids wreak havoc on the body. Was it the stress of increased cortisol that I know I had for a couple of years with Covid and the stressors of keeping family members safe and my new business afloat? I was unsure, but I continued thinking about all these possibilities. What I knew for sure was that learning to decrease stress would be a win-win situation.

Mental states can be conscious or unconscious. We can react emotionally to situations without knowing why we are reacting. Each mental state has a physiology associated with it—a positive or negative effect felt in the physical body. For example, the mental state of anxiety causes you to produce more stress hormones. I had been producing too many stress hormones, just like I'm sure many of you are in your fast-paced lives. We seem to be taught in our society that we can do it all.

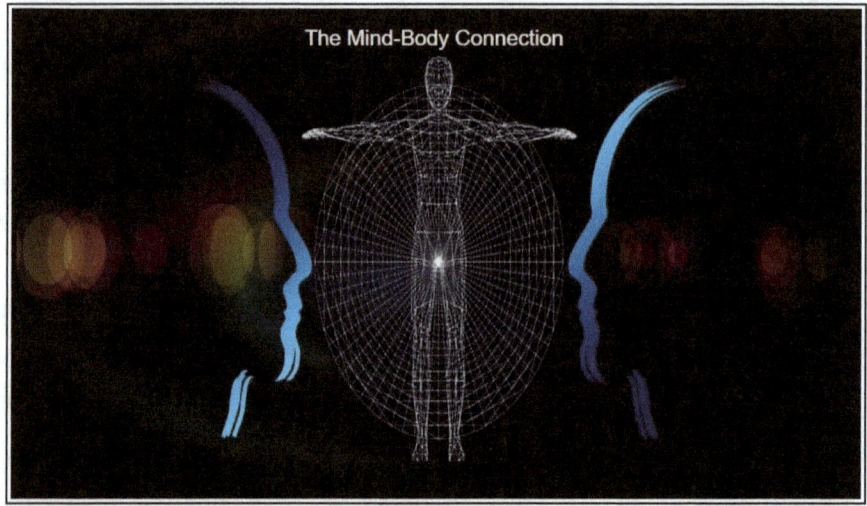

Take the time now and use this blank space in the book to create goals to help with your mind-body connection. Some examples may be changing your self-talk and noticing more instead of judging yourself, people, or events. Look for more positive patterns to enhance your life.

CHAPTER 21

Reducing Stress

Most people agree that minimizing stress in your daily life is positive. Our world is fast-paced, and many of us learn unhealthy patterns. We may not even notice the unhealthy patterns. This chapter will help the reader find ways to make some small changes in their daily life.

Ways to Decrease Stress

- *Change your thoughts*

I have always been proud of my work ethic and thought this was one of my greatest strengths. I have stamina and endurance and will get a project done no matter what it takes. However, as I have mentioned, this pattern was not suiting me well now that I needed to take it easy. I needed to learn to slow down and not be so motivated to get everything done that day.

I had to learn not to always be doing *one more thing*. I would not sit down at night until I had everything done on my list. I had to learn to take more breaks and that everything on my list may not get done. I learned that I needed to make my list about half of what it used to be. I had never really known how to do this and reduce the load until I got the acoustic neuroma. My kids did more to help each other, and they would do the cooking, or my husband would cook. All the essential things were getting done in the household, and most were not done by me anymore. Certain extracurricular activities were dropped. If someone did not want to do an activity, we subtracted it from the daily routine list.

- ### *Talk less and be more present*

I started to notice that I talked less. I used to really enjoy talking and socializing, but something had changed. I spent a lot of energy listening to others, and I may say something short and concise to contribute but not long explanations. This was also because it takes more energy for me to listen and block out the tinnitus from my head. I was listening more and focusing less on what I wanted to say.

- ### *Embrace mindfulness*

Bringing yourself to the present moment instead of thinking ahead or about the past. It can break cycles of stressful thoughts when you focus on the present, the breeze in the air, the sunset, or your child's laughter. Seeing things as they are, not good or bad, and without judgment.

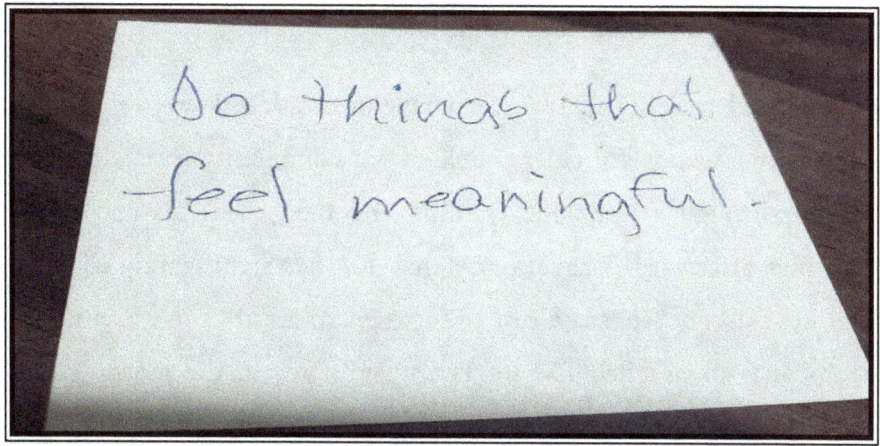

Decreasing my daily obligations is most helpful to me in being more mindful. It is hard to be mindful when you are running at such a fast pace.

- *Give yourself permission to relax*

Learn to not set the bar so high with your endeavors. Having a good work ethic is a positive characteristic, but make sure to have balance by allowing yourself time to relax and stress less.

- *Explore transcendental meditation* ™

I completed training in transcendental meditation. I was referred to meet with a wonderful older couple in our community trained in TM. I went through a weeklong training and then check-ins and group meetings afterward. I have to say that TM has significantly changed my life. I do not feel as *on edge* even when stressful things occur. The protocol is to practice TM for twenty minutes in the morning and twenty minutes in the evening. Sitting and repeating the mantra word assigned to me makes me feel less stressed and more at peace. It has even helped me sleep better and through the night. My memory seems better, and I feel more organized in my thoughts after a session of meditation. TM helps to balance my nervous system so my mind and body can relax and rest.

- *Color mandalas*

I find coloring mandalas to be helpful. Mandalas are an artistic representation of higher thought and deeper meaning. It originated in India and can promote balance and aid in meditation. Mandalas are equal and balanced on both sides, creating a feeling of balance and congruity when one adds colors or patterns to the mandala.

I have a favorite Mandala book that is not too intricate or simplistic. I have purchased other mandala books but will return to this one for myself and my clients.

Fincher, Susanne F. (2004); *Coloring Mandalas 2: For Balance, Harmony, and Spiritual Well-Being* (1st ed.). Shambhala Publications, Inc.

- *Draw or paint for recreation*

Drawing and painting is an outlet to express one's thoughts and feelings.

- *Keep health appointments*

Appointments are now mostly for health reasons, not aesthetics. In previous years, I had started going to dermatologist appointments because I was worried about sunspots appearing on my face and wanted to decrease the spots to appear younger. Now, I go to the dermatologist to monitor my lichen planus to ensure it is not becoming cancerous. An aging body means you are still living.

- *Celebrate or focus on the good times*

I learned to really enjoy the good days and moments and be more grateful when things were going well. It was hard to predict how I may feel or be functioning the next day.

My forty-seventh birthday

- *Practice patience*

I was learning to be more patient with myself and others. I was accepting the things that I could not change and stopped hitting my head against a brick wall, trying to control what was not in my control.

- *Explore massage therapy*

Massage can increase vagal tone and decrease blood pressure. It can help decrease anxiety tremendously and help the entire body, from head to toe, relax.

- *Improve vagal tone*

The vagus nerve is an information network that carries information from the body to the brain and from brain to body, the mind and body connection.

When we nourish and improve the tone of our vagus nerve, we enjoy greater contentment and ability to connect, less pain and anxiety, and improved sleep patterns.

Ways to improve vagal tone include

- breathwork

- cold exposure

- exercise

- meditation

- laughter

- singing

- relaxation exercises

- *Spend time with pets*

I like to spend more time with my dog. She is a Wheaten Terrier and is so expressive when she looks at me. It is easy to make her happy with a walk. Dogs are the best teachers of mindfulness and being in the moment. I try to take her on a daily walk because it helps her get out her energy and it helps me with my balance. Pets can decrease loneliness, increase feelings of social support, and boost mood.

- ***Feel more content in your home***

I also noticed that the more I've stayed home, the happier I seem to be. Home is more peaceful, and I can read and write and not be overstimulated. I have enjoyed staying home much more since my brain surgery. It is less overwhelming for me. My family started eating more meals at home and having more family movie nights to just *stay in*.

- *Create collages*

Making collages can be peaceful and meaningful. Cutting out pictures or phrases from magazines or other sources to create a unique visual representation can be fulfilling. This process can be calming when a person focuses on what is soothing to them, future goals, and things they are grateful for, and it helps them explore future dreams and endeavors. It becomes a visual representation of how a person communicates, thinks, or feels.

- *Remember the good times*

Focusing on great memories in your life is helpful to feel at peace and grateful. Creating a photo wall or other photo area can help people focus on their best times in life while going through more stressful times.

- *Practice gratitude*

Gratitude is a shield from negativity, rewires your brain, and makes you happier.

I sent a holiday card to the UCSD Medical team, thanking them for the surgery and the great care I received at their hospital and under the care of their very experienced surgeons. I also wrote thank you notes to everyone who brought us food and other gifts.

- **_Find your inner strength_**

My paternal grandparents were first-generation immigrants from Finland. The Finns have a term, "Sisu," to describe a special strength to overcome adversity; an almost magical quality...a combination of stamina, perseverance, courage, and determination held in reserve for tough times. It is important to find your Sisu to get through hard times. I have had many days where I felt knocked down and trampled over, but I have always been able to get back up and see clearly again. My extended family gave me this necklace at our Arnio Family Reunion over the summer. The wording is from the necklace packaging.

Sisu

A special strength and persistent resolve to continue and overcome in times of adversity.

- *Journal*

I started journaling more often. This helped me with authoring this book and writing my thoughts down on paper first in my journal. The journal that works the best for me has a space for the date and journal entry number at the top of the page. I feel more productive if I see the journal entry number, which seems more structured and focused for me. Try to journal incorporating the feeling words happiness, sadness, disgust, fear, surprise, and anger to fully express your emotional experience.

- *Stretch*

Stretching activities loosen up tight muscles and incorporate breathing to help feel more of a sense of calm. Stretching increases serotonin levels, which helps stabilize our mood, reduce stress, and make us feel good overall.

- *Take one day at a time*

Do not focus on all the "what ifs." Most of the time, these worries do not come true, and you end up ruining the present, ruminating on the possibilities of bad things.

- *Engage in humor*

Laughter can reduce stress hormones and expresses hope, optimism, and joy. Memes can make me chuckle and not take life so seriously. Spend time with people who are fun and make you laugh.

- *Participate in mental health counseling*

Meeting regularly with a mental health professional who hears and understands your situation can reduce stress and anxiety. Feel your feelings and learn to accept what you cannot change. Therapists can help you notice patterns in your life. People learn to combat negative thoughts and learn to speak to yourself in your head as you would speak to a friend, positive self-talk.

- *Self-care*

- Indoor plants increase calm

- Find a hobby or something you are passionate about

- Document your gratefulness in a journal, collage, painting

- Spend time with your pet

- Do something nice for someone else

- Massage

- Light candles

- Open curtains for natural light

- Eat good food

- Drink a lot of water, especially in the morning

- Go outside

- Get together with your friends

- Set aside some time each day to unwind and relax

- *Notice the good in the world or in your day*

Life can be hard, but what were some of the good moments? Spend time thinking of positive memories and things you are proud of. Recall the activities that make you smile or laugh and increase those activities.

- *Listen to your body*

I have been starting to listen more to my body. If my head is hurting and I feel like I cannot be out working for a full day, I am making accommodations. I used to just push through this, but I am now learning that if I rest when I feel like I need to rest, I have a better overall result.

When I was in Steamboat skiing four months after surgery, it was the end of the day, and I was getting tired. We were traveling down a steep hill. I fell onto my backside and started to panic because I felt dizzy. I was not sure why I was up so high skiing. I enjoyed the whole trip except for that moment. I was able to make it down the hill slowly and stated that it was my last run for the day. I was learning to listen to my body.

- *Spend time around a body of water*

Being around water has a positive impact on things related to mental restoration. Spend some time by the lake, river, ocean, pool, or fountain.

- *Use your experience to help others or learn from others*

Helping others connects us to other people and gives us a sense of purpose. Individuals feel more supported and understood when they know others are going through the same situation—a *sense of community* with others going through the same thing as you: universality.

When I was first diagnosed, I talked to a friend of a friend who had gone through acoustic neuroma surgery, and she gave me advice and explained her experience. This helped me feel understood and more confident that I could also make it through this predicament.

I was put in contact with a young male college student who had a brain tumor, different than an acoustic neuroma, but he needed to have brain surgery soon. I talked with him about his feelings about having a tumor in his head, and he was able to explain that he had the same feelings and stress of something growing in one's body and what to do to take care of it.

I was contacted by an older woman from the Pacific Northwest who was diagnosed years ago with an acoustic neuroma, and she was deciding to go ahead and get the surgery. I recommended UC at San Diego and told her that I did not think my surgery experience could have been any better. I sent her pictures of the campus housing and recommended what seemed to help the most and least after my surgery. This really helped me feel useful, and I was here to help others in the same predicament. She stayed connected and later sent me pictures of her and her daughter in California getting the surgery completed.

The Acoustic Neuroma Association (www.anausa.org) is a great organization that provides education and support to people with acoustic neuromas. I recently became a peer mentor to help others newly diagnosed with acoustic neuromas. Volunteers encourage and support AN patients via telephone, email, or video chat. Mentors are located across the United States, and I am the first mentor in South Dakota. I had my first official ANA mentor-mentee call in January 2024, and I found it very rewarding.

CHAPTER 22

The Miracle

At about a year and three months out from brain surgery, I went back to my audiologist with thoughts of trying out a hearing aid, specifically a hearing aid with a masker. This was recommended by UCSD staff since I was still battling more fatigue and tinnitus than I found tolerable. At first, I did not want to be a young person wearing a hearing aid, but I changed my mind after testing one out for a couple of weeks.

I was ecstatic, elated, and euphoric about my new experience in my head and my daily life! The hearing aid was like a supercharge for me. I could work, come home, make supper, and attend my kids' activities. I could even stay up late reading or doing other projects. I was amazed by the difference this little device made in my quality of life.

My hearing actually wasn't that bad; I only have mild to moderate hearing loss, but the masker seemed to be the missing piece of the puzzle. It takes the internal noise out of my head (like a vacuum cleaner), so I could concentrate on the present. Hallelujah! Was my quality of life going to get back to pre-tumor functioning? I sure did hope so. I wrote in this book for hours on end, trying to finish it so I could be productive and energetic again.

About a month down the road, the hearing seemed not to be doing the job as well anymore. Again, I was napping more and could not concentrate as long. I went back for my hearing aid check and my audiologist adjusted the hearing aid. Again, I was back to my energetic self, functioning all day without a problem.

Another month went by, and I was not feeling up to par again. I was unsure if I had a sinus cold or if my hearing aid was the culprit. My audiologist adjusted the hearing aid again; the next day, I felt better again. Wow. I did not want a hearing aid because I did not want to look like an elderly person, but the truth be told, it was helping me be more active like an energetic younger person.

I learned that I must be more careful when wearing this hearing aid. I could not whip my shirt off in a rush to change clothes because the hearing aid would fly across the room. I was also raking leaves on a beautiful fall day and carrying heavy lawn bags to the driveway. I found my hearing aid on the driveway and did not even realize I had lost it. Hearing aids are not cheap, and this one was over $2000. I am trying to be more careful with this little miracle device. It has been a lifesaver for me at one year and four months out from surgery.

CHAPTER 23

Post Traumatic Growth

ost-traumatic growth is growth or changes after a highly challenging or traumatic event. Experiencing a traumatic event can have a transformational role in personality among certain individuals.

In my case, this has been true. I have always liked my job as a mental health counselor, but after twenty-plus years, I feel a bit of a spark and passion regarding a fresh writing career. I have always wanted to write and read. This past year, since my surgery, my love of reading has increased even more. I feel productive when I finish a new book and usually find something helpful in each book—a statement, a quote, or a shared experience. I am not sure if I would have ever started writing without this push from a medical issue. I was comfortable in my routine and found my current career fulfilling. This unplanned detour is pushing me to take this leap to writing.

I wanted to help others who are newly diagnosed with acoustic neuromas.

I struggled with trying to find balance again after the surgery. I feel good when I am productive and working hard. I have now given myself permission to do something different. I do not feel good anymore after a fully booked day at my office. I have always liked providing for myself and contributing financially to my family. Growing up, my mother encouraged me to be able to provide for myself. In high school, even though my family was not poor, I decided to work at the grocery store at night. During our community's summer celebration, I worked at the grocery store and vendor stands until after midnight. This was all self-imposed. I found this fulfilling, being a hard worker.

After getting married in my twenties, my husband was in school for longer than I did. He is one year younger than me. I felt proud when we rented our first apartment in St Louis, Missouri, and I could pay the rent and our expenses because he was still in graduate school. When we bought our first house, again, he was doing his rotations for school, and I felt proud that the more hours I worked a day, the better we would sit financially. I know that money is not everything, but life can sure become stressful when there is not enough to pay the bills. This pattern of working more had always worked out for me in the past, but it no longer was working for me a year out in recovering from the surgery. I decided to give myself permission to do something else—create a new pattern. I needed to take the leap and see where I would end up.

My first leap is authoring this book. I think this book will be helpful to those who are newly diagnosed with this condition, those who love them, and those trying to find a good quality of life living with their symptoms after their chosen treatment.

My next leap is giving myself permission to work three days at my office and have two days at home to work on writing projects. I arranged to rent my office space to another therapist in town two days a week. This is a safety plan in case I am as ill as last winter with all the weather changes and colds. I will have another provider to help pay the mortgage on the building. If I am not as sick this coming winter, the extra money will help pay off the mortgage on my business building more quickly. It is a win-win situation that I produced trying to plan for winter and finances. I had to be more flexible in my thinking, adapt, and create new patterns.

Bibliotherapy

I plan to write more nonfiction books on other topics that are of interest to me, perhaps the pros and cons of social media, self-concept, parenting issues, meditation, relationship issues, and finding meaning in life. Writing my first book has been very exciting. I have joy in thinking of new ideas and jotting them down on paper so I can write about them later. Often, on walks, I think of a new idea and put it in my phone to write more about when I get back home. I set a deadline to have the second revision of this book back to my editor by my forty-eighth birthday, and I accomplished that goal, feeling a sense of mastery. My middle son has helped me tremendously with the computer issues of sending a large manuscript back and forth to my editor, who resides in Canada. My middle son also helped redevelop the memes and images in the document. This has brought us closer, and he seems to be excited about the book being published.

I have a particular love for using bibliotherapy to help children through specific stressors. Child therapists select specific therapeutic books to read with children. The character in the book is most likely going through struggles similar to the client. It is written to help them understand that all feelings are okay, there are various hardships in life, and there are ways to change thinking and coping to get through life stressors to be more resilient. Reading has certainly helped me through many struggles and finding a sense of purpose and peace in this busy world. It has also shaped me into being a strong, resilient woman. Many people have gone through worse than I have. Reading can help change your perspective.

Over the years, I have made a list of books I would like to write for children and families. I am excited to get started on books with several different themes for children:

- Parents separating or divorcing

- Relocating

- Bullying

- Decreasing impulsivity

- Worries

- Courage

- A friend moving away

- Co-parenting through separation or divorce

- Learning to be more flexible in thinking

- Social skills

- Having more than one feeling at the same time

- Illness

- Death and grieving

Post-traumatic growth has also helped me gain a unique perspective on the brain tumor. So, are there any positive points of having this acoustic neuroma discovered at age forty-six, in my case?

- I am so grateful that my children were older (sixteen, thirteen, and ten) when I was diagnosed with acoustic neuroma. It would be much more difficult to go through the surgery or even the symptoms if your children are incredibly young and crying, yelling, and not letting the parent nap when needed. I was blessed that my boys were old enough to understand that I was going through something hard and that I could not have loud and overwhelming things around because my head would hurt even more.

- I am thankful that my husband is so intelligent and detail-oriented. He researched for hours on end regarding which medical team to go with for my treatment. He stood by whatever decision I made after all the facts were presented. He had MRIs sent numerous times to medical teams. He dealt with the insurance company, getting referrals here and there. He paid huge bills out of nowhere because it was a new year, and we had to reach our deductible again. We were steadfast and strong.

- I am lucky to have my parents and sister/brother-in-law, who dropped everything and came to California to provide support and company during this challenging time. I know it was extremely hard for them as well to see their child go through this. My sister and brother-in-law were wonderful as well. My sister has been trying to ensure everyone in the family is doing well. At the time of writing this book, both of my parents had Covid, and my sister had been tending to them day and night. Covid is when all of this started for me, so I pray that they recover fully and do not have any lingering or permanent issues from Covid.

- I was awestruck by the generosity, love, and support from friends and relatives through this tough time in my life. During my recovery period, they set up a food train to feed my family while I recovered. I received gifts and treats by my front door, and beautiful fall flowers were waiting for me on my doorstep when I returned from California. I could not believe the good people in the world were trying to lift me during this tough time. This was amazing, and I could not believe all the love being sent from down the street or across the country for my recovery.

A person's mindset has everything to do with having an enjoyable life after a major life-changing event. All the help and support that I had from family and friends helped me with my strength. But I had to decide as to how I was going to chase after life again. I could give up or come back swinging and do everything possible to improve my quality of life. It is up to you as the reader to choose. There is a new normal after an upheaval. You can view it in a negative light or try to find the small glimmers and focus on those as much as possible. You can find your passion or path again, maybe in a new and improved way.

Glimmers in life are the opposite of hardships. They spark joy and make you feel childlike again with wonder. They positively affect mental health and put us at ease, allowing us to feel safe and regulate our nervous system. They help us feel hope about ourselves, the world, or humankind. An example of a glimmer in my life was when my group of friends in my book club met for dinner, and our friend talked about how she had decorated a large tree in her yard to remember her four-month-old, deceased daughter years ago. The tree was not lighting up well anymore due to the squirrels chewing at the wires over the years and the passage of time.

We organized a group of friends to pool our resources to rent a bucket truck and spend a Saturday redecorating the tree. We could not do anything about the fact that she and her husband had lost their baby daughter, but we knew the significance of this tree, and working together, we could help make this happen for them. Working together on a common goal to produce joy was a wonderful feeling.

Walking with my dog the other day, I spotted a beautiful vine with changing leaves on an old chimney. The chimney was cracked and repaired, and the leaves held strong to the bricks, creating a beautiful vine and autumn nature scene. All the leaves were necessary to create the beautiful vine, similar to how our experiences create who we are as human beings. Leaves change colors and die, and new leaves are formed. The repaired chimney and bricks are more beautiful with character from years of wear and tear. Some cracks can be repaired, and the beauty and function can return. Our relationships, experiences, joy, and pain shape who we are and how we see the world. Life is an intricate and amazing journey, and we learn how to adapt along the way.

I have grown as a person and become more resilient and courageous to move forward with change. Now, I focus on being mindful of how I spend my days. The time we have left is a limited resource. Are there areas where you want to grow, learn, or change? What would these be, and what is holding you back in these areas?

A Year of Firsts

Six Weeks Out

Back to work part-time

Two Months Out

I Flew by myself to conference in St. Louis

Close friends dining on "The Hill"

St Louis Arch

David Crenshaw
(endorsements on back cover)

Juliet Fortino
(endorsements on back cover)

Four Months Out

Ski Trip to Steamboat

Seven Months Out

Snorkeling in Jamaica with my family

Eleven Months Out

Pink Concert in Minneapolis

Famous People with Acoustic Neuromas

Mark Ruffalo – An American actor and three-time Oscar nominee, best known as the Hulk in the *Avengers*.

Kelly Stafford – Wife of Los Angeles Rams quarterback Matthew Stafford.

Alan Alda – Actor, author, and activist; passion for science spurred him to host the PBS show Scientific American Frontiers.

Sharon Osbourne – TV personality, author, music manager, businesswoman, and promoter.

Pat DiNizio – Lead singer and songwriter for the Smithereens.

Marvin Hamlisch – Renowned composer and conductor.

Music

Music helps us feel emotions, heal, and feel understood. Below is a list of songs I identified with during the acoustic neuroma discovery and treatment.

Pink	Trustfall
	Turbulence
	All I Know So Far
Tim McGraw	Live Like You Were Dying
Andra Day	Rise Up
AJR	Break My Face
Harry Stiles	As It Was
	(Cait Martin's rendition is top notch)
Rachel Platten	Fight Song
Katy Perry	Roar
Kane Brown, Katelyn Brown	Thank God
Avicii	Wake Me Up
AJR	Way Less Sad
Em Beihold	Numb Little Bug
The Doors	Break On Through
Tesla	We're No Good Together

Appreciation

I wish to thank all my doctors/providers for helping and guiding me through the past two years.

- University of California at San Diego

- Creekside Medical Clinic

- West River ENT

- ProMotion Physical Therapy

- Transcendental Meditation© Rapid City

- Dharma Wellness Institute

- Thrive Acupuncture

- Rapid City Medical Center Dermatology and Gastroenterology

- Monument Dermatology

- Thorn Counseling

- Alternative Health Care Center

- LMB Therapy

Thank You, Reader

I am incredibly honored that you have read my first book.

If you have enjoyed my book, please go to Amazon

and leave a review as soon as possible.

Here are the steps:

1. Log into your Amazon account

2. Go to Account Details at the top of the screen and click on *Your Orders*.

3. Find the book you want to review and select *Product Review*.

4. Give the book a five-star review!

Thank you!

I have included a drawing and letter from my youngest son on the following pages. My three sons have been very supportive, and we have all grown in numerous ways through this challenging experience.

Going From Pain To GAIN

A drawing and note from my youngest son, age eleven.

Mom,

I think you are amazing and you will get shiny medals on your books. You are a warrior. You have grown so much since your surgery. You are one tough mom. From having babies to getting hearing aids you fight through everything and make so many people happy. Being a childrens book writer will have challenges, but because of what you've done so far I know it will be no problem for my supermom.

You have a shining heart of gold that shines upon us and makes us bright.

Dalton

Resources

Kacker, Ashutosh, Dan Brennan, and Tara Novick. "Acoustic Neuroma What Is Acoustic Neuroma?" UC San Diego Health Health Library. The StayWell Company, January 2, 2023. https://myhealth.ucsd.edu/Library/DiseasesConditions/Adult/Otolaryngology/85,P00438.

Mayo Clinic Health System. "Coping Tips for a Serious Diagnosis," n.d. https://www.mayoclinichealthsystem.org/hometown-health/speaking-of-health/8-tips-for-coping-with-a-serious-diagnosis.

www.ingramcontent.com/pod-product-compliance
Lightning Source LLC
Chambersburg PA
CBHW070658130626
46553CB00005B/1757